ENGLISH
DICTIONARY of ABBREVIATIONS
used in the European Union

FRANÇAIS
DICTIONNAIRE des SIGLES
utilisés dans l'Union européenne

DEUTSCH
ABKÜRZUNGSWÖRTERBUCH
Europäische Union

РУССКИЙ
СЛОВАРЬ СОКРАЩЕНИЙ,
применяемых в Европейском Союзе

D1664260

1999

Abkürzungswörterbuch Europäische Union

© European Commission, 1997
© Jourist Verlag, 1999

Bestelladresse:
Jourist Verlags GmbH
Wendenstr. 435,
20537 Hamburg
Tel.: 040-210 98 29 0, Fax: 040-210 98 29 3
E-mail: jourist@aol.com
Internet: http://www.jourist.de

ISBN 3-932864-60-3

Contents
Tables des matières
Inhalt
Содержание

FOREWORD

The development of integration in Europe and, in particular, the activities of the European Union (EU), has given rise to a multitude of new organizations, programmes and forms of co-operation as well as new terms which in official documents and literature are accompanied by abbreviations, often poorly known not only to the general public but also to specialists. The Fourlingual Dictionary of Abbreviations, brought to the attention of the readers, is an attempt to at least fill partially this gap.

The Dictionary lists more than 500 entries concerning both the internal activities of the European Union and its relations with third countries, regional (first of all European) and international organizations. In composing the Dictionary the authors have taken into account the abbreviations of the terms which have appeared in recent years as a result of the development of co-operation between the EU and Russia and other countries of the Commonwealth of Independent States (CIS). For the first time in such a dictionary the Russian-alphabet abbreviations of the terms as well as their definitions and explanations in Russian are included.

We hope the Dictionary will be a useful guide for public servants, businessmen, researchers, professors, students and all those who are interested in the issues of integration and co-operation in Europe.

How to use the Dictionary?

The entries are arranged according to the English version of the abbreviations given in alphabetical order. Inside each entry alongside the abbreviation and its full form in the English language are included the respective equivalents in French, German and Russian. The dash "-" means that there is no commonly used abbreviation in the corresponding language.

To facilitate searching for the required entry the Dictionary incorporates the general index of all Latin-alphabet abbreviations with the reference numbers assigned to them, as well as a separate index of Russian-alphabet abbreviations.

The abbreviations of the names of the EU Member countries and those of their national currencies are given in the supplement.

Explanations are offered in those cases where the translation into Russian is insufficient for understanding and may lead to misinterpretations. The Russian abbreviation "EC" marks the institutes, programmes, forms of action or agreements of the European Union.

	Entry number 167			
English abbreviation	EN	**EEA**	**European Economic Area**	English term
French abbreviation	FR	**EEE**	**Espace économique europeén**	French equivalent
German abbreviation	DE	**EWR**	**Europäisher Wirtschaftsraum**	Germanequivalent
Russian abbreviation	RU	**ЕЭП**	**Европейское экономическое пространство**	Russianequivalent
			включает страны ЕС и ЕАСТ	Definition in Russian

As sources of the information the authors have used the official documents of the European Union (Treaties establishing the European Communities, reports of the European Commission etc.), bulletins of the Agency "Europe", articles of the "Evropa"magazine published by the Delegation of the European Commission in Moscow and reference books and dictionaries including those issued in the EU.

AVANT-PROPOS

Le développement de l'intégration en Europe et surtout les activités de l''Union européenne (UE) ont fait naître une multitude de nouveaux organismes, programmes et formes de coopération, ainsi que de termes nouveaux qui sont désignés dans les documents officiels et la littérature par des sigles souvent peu connus non seulement du grand public mais aussi des spécialistes. Le Dictionnaire de sigles quadrilinque que nous présentons aux lecteurs est destiné à combler, au moins partiellement, cette lacune.

Le Dictionnaire contient plus de 500 entrées qui se rapportent tant aux activités intérieurs de l'Union européenne qu'à ses relations avec les pays tiers, les organisations régionales (avant tout européennes) et internationales. Au cours de la préparation du Dictionnaire les auteurs ont tenu compte des sigles de termes parus ces derniers temps suite à l'extention de la coopération de l'Union européenne avec la Russie et d'autres pays-membres de la Communauté des Etats Indépendants (CEI).

C'est pour la première fois que nous avons inclus dans un ouvrage de ce genre des sigles de termes russes ainsi que leurs définitions et les explications en langue russe.

Nous espérons que le présent Dictionnaire sera un guide utile à l'administration publique, aux hommes d'affaires, chercheurs, professeurs, étudiants et à tous ceux qui s'intéressent aux problèmes d'intégration et de coopération en Europe.

Comment utiliser ce Dictionnaire?

Les entrées sont rangées dans l'ordre alphabétique en se basant sur la version anglaise des sigles. Chaque entrée comprend aux côtés du sigle anglais et son déchiffrement des équivalents respectifs en langues française, allemande et russe. Le signe "-" signifie qu'il n'y a pas de sigle (courant) dans la langue concernée.

Pour faciliter la recherche de l'entrée nécessaire le Dictionnaire est muni de l'index général de toutes les abréviations anglaises, françaises et allemandes mentionnées dans l'ordre de l'alphabet latin avec des numéros de référence, et de l'index séparé des sigles russes.

Les sigles des noms des Etats-membres de l'Union européenne et ceux des dénominations de leurs monnaies nationales sont présentés en supplément.

Dans les cas où la traduction en russe n'est pas suffisante pour la compréhention précise et peut provoquer quelque doute les auteurs donnent des explications ou précisions nécessaires. Le sigle russe *"EC"* se réfère aux institutions, programmes, formes d'actions ou accords de l'Union européenne.

		Numero de l'entrée 167		
Sigle anglais	EN	**EEA**	**European Economic Area**	Terme anglais
Sigle français	FR	**EEE**	**Espace économique européen**	Equivalent français
Sigle allemand	DE	**EWR**	**Europäischer Wirtschaftsraum**	Equivalent allemand
Sigle russe Equivalent russe	RU	**ЕЭП**	**Европейское экономическое пространство** *включает страны ЕС и ЕАСТ*	Explication en langue russe

Les auteurs ont utilisé comme sources d'information les documents officiels de l'Union européenne (traités instituant les Communautés européennes, rapports de la Commission européenne etc.), bulletins de l'Agence "Europe", articles de la revue "Evropa", publiée par la Représentation de la Commission européenne à Moscou, ouvrages de référence et dictionnaires, y compris ceux édités dans l'Union européenne.

VORWORT

Die Entwicklung der Integration in Europa und insbesondere die Tätigkeit der Europäischen Union haben eine grosse Anzahl neuer Organisationen, Programme und Formen der Zusammenarbeit sowie der neuer Fachausdrücke ins Leben gerufen, die in offiziellen Dokumenten und Literatur mit Abkürzungen gekennzeichnet sind, die häufig nicht nur der Öffentlichkeit, sondern auch den Spezialisten wenig bekannt sind. Das vorliegende viersprächige Wörterbuch der Abkürzungen soll die Lücke füllen.

Das Wörterbuch enthält mehr als 500 Abkürzungsblöcke, die mit der inneren Tätigkeit der Europäischen Union verbunden sind, und Abkürzungen, die Beziehungen der EU mit Drittländern und mit regionalen (vor allem) europäischen und internationalen Organisationen betreffen. Bei dem Verfassen des Wörterbuchs werden die Abkürzungen der Fachausdrücke berücksichtigt, die in letzter Zeit infolge der Entwicklung der Zusammenarbeit der EU mit Russland und anderen Ländern der Gemeinschaft der Unabhängigen Republiken mehr und mehr Anwendung gefunden haben. Zum ersten Male sind in diesem Wörterbuch die russischen Abkürzungen der Fachausdrücke, ihre Definition und notwendige Erklärungen in russischer Sprache angegeben.

Wir hoffen, dass disees Wörterbuch eine nützliche Informationsquelle für Staatsbeamte, Unternehmer, Wissenschaftler, Professoren, Studenten und andere sein wird, die sich mit den Problemen der Integration und der Zusammenarbeit in Europa auseinandersetzen.

Hinweise zur Benutzung des Wörterbuch

Die in ihrer englischen Version zitierten Einträge folgen dem lateinischen Alphabet. Innerhalb des Blocks neben der Abkürzung und deren englischer Übersetzung ist die französische, deutsche und russische Entsprechung angeführt. Auslassungszeichen bedeuten dass eine Abkürzung in dieser Sprache fehlt.

Das Wörterbuch enthält ein Abkürzungsverzeichnis. Die Abkürzungen sind in englischer, französischer und deutscher Sprache, in der Reihenfolge des lateinischen Alphabets mit der laufenden Nummer des Blocks und im folgenden russischen Abkürzungsverzeichnis angegeben, was die Suche erleichtert.

Ergänzend sind die Abkürzungen der Bennenungen der Mitgliedsländer der EU sowie die Bezeichnungen derer nationalen Währungen gennant.

Erklärungen sind in den Fällen angegeben, wo die Übersetzung ins Russicher ungenügend für das Verstehen ist bzw. zu verschiedenen Interpretation führen könnte. Mit der russischen Abkürzung *"EC"* sind die Organe, Programme, Tätigkeitsformen und Verträge der Europäischen Union bezeichnet.

Nummer
des Blocks

	167			
Englische Abkürzung	EN	**EEA**	**European Economic Area**	Englische Fachausdrücke
Französische Abkürzung	FR	**EEE**	**Espace économique européen**	Französishe Äquivalent
Deutsche Abkürzung	DE	**EWR**	**Europäischer Wirtschaftsraum**	Deutsches Äquivalent
Russische Abkürzung	RU	**ЕЭП**	**Европейское экономиское пространство**	Russisches Äquivalent
			включает страны ЕС и EACT	Erklärung in russischer Sprache

Als Informationsquellen sind offizielle Dokumente der Europäischen Union (Gründungsverträge, Vorträge der Europäischen Kommission usw.) genutzt, sowie das Bulletin der Agentur "Europa", Artikel aus der Zeitschrift "Evropa", die von der Vertretung der Europäischen Kommission in Moskau herausgegeben wird, sowie in der EU verlegte Hand- und Wörterbücher.

ПРЕДИСЛОВИЕ

Развитие интеграции в Европе и, в особенности, деятельность Европейского Союза (ЕС), вызвали к жизни множество новых организаций, программ и форм сотрудничества, а также новых терминов, которые в официальных документах и литературе обозначаются сокращениями, часто малоизвестными не только широкой публике, но и специалистам. Предлагаемый Четырехязычный Словарь сокращений призван, хотя бы частично, восполнить этот пробел.

Словарь содержит более 500 блоков сокращений, связанных как с внутренней деятельностью Европейского Союза, так и с его отношениями с третьими странами, с региональными (прежде всего европейскими) и международными организациями. При составлении Словаря учтены сокращения терминов, появившихся в последнее время в результате развития сотрудничества ЕС с Россией и другими странами Содружества независимых государств (СНГ). Впервые в подобного рода словарях приводятся русские сокращения терминов, даются их определения и необходимые пояснения на русском языке.

Мы надеемся, что Словарь станет полезным справочником для государственных учреждений, предпринимателей, научных работников, преподавателей, студентов и всех тех, кто интересуется проблемами интеграции и сотрудничества в Европе.

Как пользоваться Словарем?

Блоки сокращений даются в алфавитном порядке английских сокращений. Внутри каждого блока, наряду с сокращениями и его расшифровкой на английском языке, приводятся французские, немецкие и русские эквиваленты. Знак "-" означает отсутствие устоявшихся сокращений в соответствующем языке.

В целях облегчения поиска необходимого блока Словарь содержит сводный перечень сокращений на английском, французском и немецком языках, расположенных в порядке латинского алфавита с указанием порядкового номера блока, и отдельный перечень русских сокращений.

Дополнительно приведены сокращения названий государств-членов ЕС, а также их национальных валют.

Пояснения даются в тех случаях, когда перевод на русский язык недостаточен для понимания какого-либо термина и может дать повод для различных толкований. Русским сокращением "ЕС" отмечены органы, программы, формы действий и соглашений Европейского Союза.

	Номер блока 167			
Английское сокращение	EN	**EEA**	**European Economic Area**	Английский термин
Французское сокращение	FR	**EEE**	**Espace économique européen**	Французский эквивалент
Немецкое сокращение	DE	**EWR**	**Europäischer Wirtschaftsraum**	Немецкий эквивалент
Русское сокращение	RU	**ЕЭП**	**Европейское экономическое пространство**	Русский эквивалент
			включает страны ЕС и ЕАСТ	Пояснение на русском языке

В качестве источников информации авторы использовали официальные документы Европейского Союза (договоры, учреждающие Европейские сообщества, доклады Европейской Комиссии и др.); бюллетени Агентства "Европа"'; статьи из журнала "Европа", издаваемого Представительством Европейской Комиссии в Москве; справочники и словари, в том числе опубликованные в ЕС.

CORPUS

CORPUS

KORPUS

СОКРАЩЕНИЯ И ИХ РАСШИФРОВКА

EN	**English**
FR	**Français**
DE	**Deutsch**
RU	**Русский**

1
EN	AASM; AAMS	Associated African States and Madagascar; Associated African and Madagascar States
FR	EAMA	Etats africains et malgache associés
DE	AASM	Assoziierte afrikanische Staaten und Madagaskar
RU	-	ассоциированные страны Африки и Мадагаскар

18 стран, участвовавших в I и II Яундских конвенциях об ассоциации с ЕЭС

2
EN	ACA	accession compensatory amounts
FR	MCA	montants compensatoires adhésion
DE	-	Beitrittsausgleichsbeträge
RU	-	вступительные компенсационные суммы

доплаты и скидки, применяемые при расчетах между старыми и новыми членами ЕС с целью компенсации разницы в уровнях цен на сельскохозяйственные товары

3
EN	ACE	Actions by the Community relating to the environment
FR	ACE	Actions communautaires pour l'environnement
DE	GUA	Gemeinschaftliche Umweltaktionen
RU	-	План действий Сообщества по охране окружающей среды

4
EN	ACE	Association of European Community Airlines
FR	ACE	Association des compagnies aériennes de la Communauté européenne
DE	-	Assoziation der Flugzeugwerke der EG
RU	-	Ассоциация авиационных компаний Европейского сообщества

5
EN	ACE	Community action for co-operation in the field of economics
FR	ACE	Action communautaire de coopération dans le domaine de la science économique
DE	ACE	Aktion der Gemeinschaft für Zusammenarbeit im Bereich der Wirtschaftswissenschaften
RU	-	План действий Сообщества по сотрудничеству в области экономической науки

осуществляется в рамках программ ФАРЕ и Тасис

6
| EN | ACM | Arab Common Market |

FR	MCA	Marché commun arabe
DE	-	Arabischer Gemeinsamermarkt
RU	AOP	Арабский общий рынок

7

EN	ACNAT	Actions by the Community relating to Nature Conservation
FR	ACNAT	Actions communautaires pour la conservation de la nature
DE	GANAT	Gemeinschaftliche Aktionen zum Naturschutz
RU	-	План действий Сообщества по сохранению природы

8

EN	ACP	African, Caribbean and Pacific States
FR	ACP	Etats d'Afrique, des Caraïbes et du Pacifique
DE	AKP	Staaten in Afrika, im karibischen Raum und im Pazifischen Ozean
RU	АКТ	страны Африки, бассейнов Карибского моря и Тихого океана
		участники Ломейских конвенций о торгово-экономических отношениях с ЕС

9

EN	ACP	Agreement relating to Community patents
FR	-	accord en matière de brevets communautaires
DE	VGP	Vereinbarung über Gemeinschaftspatente
RU	-	соглашение о патенте Сообщества

10

EN	ADN	European Agreement concerning the International Carriage of Dangerous Goods by Inland Waterway
FR	ADN	Accord européen relatif au transport international des marchandises dangereuses par voie de navigation intérieure
DE	ADN	Europäisches Übereinkommen über die internationale Beförderung gefährlicher Güter auf Binnenwasserstrassen
RU	-	Европейское соглашение о международных перевозках опасных грузов по внутренним водным путям

11

EN	ADR	European Agreement concerning the International Carriage of Dangerous Goods by Road
FR	ADR	Accord européen relatif au transport international des marchandises dangereuses par route
DE	ADR	Europäisches Übereinkommen über die internationale Beförderung gefährlicher Güter auf der Strasse

RU - Европейское соглашение о международных
автомобильных перевозках опасных грузов

12
EN AE agricultural element
FR EA élément agricole
DE - Agrarelement
RU - сельскохозяйственный элемент
часть таможенного сбора при ввозе в ЕС
переработанной сельскохозяйственной продукции

13
EN AETR European Agreement concerning the Work of Crews of
Vehicles engaged in International Road Transport
FR AETR Accord européen relatif au travail des équipages des
véhicules effectuant des transports internationaux par
route
DE AETR Europäisches Übereinkommen über die Arbeit des im
internationalen Strassenverkehr beschäftigten
Fahrpersonals
RU - Европейское соглашение об условиях работы
экипажей грузовых автомобилей, осуществляющих
международные перевозки

14
EN AGR European Agreement on Main International Traffic
Arteries
FR AGR Accord européen sur les grandes routes de trafic
international
DE AGR Europäisches Übereinkommen über die Hauptstrassen
des internationalen Verkehrs
RU - Европейское соглашение по основным
международным транспортным магистралям

15
EN AIA agricultural income aid
FR ARA aide au revenu agricole
DE - Agrareinkommen Unterstützung
RU - помощь на поддержание доходов в сельском
хозяйстве

16
EN AIP-SME Agency for the International Promotion of SMEs
FR API-PME Agence pour la promotion internationale des PME
DE API-PME Agentur zur internationalen Förderung der kleinen
und mittleren Betriebe
RU - Агентство по международному содействию мелким
и средним предприятиям

17

EN	AMS	aggregate measure of support
FR	MGS	mesure globale de soutien
DE	-	globales Subventionsmessinstrument
RU	АИП	агрегатное измерение поддержки
		суммарный показатель поддержки
		сельскохозяйственного производства

18

EN	APEC	Asia-Pacific Economic Co-operation
FR	CEAP; APEC	Coopération économique Asie-Pacifique
DE	APEC	Asiatisch-Pazifische Wirtschaftszusammenarbeit
RU	АПЕК	Азиатско-тихоокеанское экономическое
		сотрудничество

19

EN	ARE	Group of the European Radical Alliance
FR	ARE	groupe de l'Alliance radicale européenne
DE	ARE	Fraktion der Radikalen Europäischen Allianz
RU	-	группа Европейского радикального альянса
		фракция в Европейском Парламенте

20

EN	ASEAN	Association of Southeast Asian Nations
FR	ASEAN,ANASE	Association des nations de l'Asie du Sud-Est
DE	ASEAN	Verband Südostasiatischer Nationen
RU	АСЕАН	Ассоциация государств Юго-Восточной Азии

21

EN	ASEM	Asia-Europe Meeting
FR	ASEM	Rencontre Asie-Europe
DE	ASEM	Asiatisch-Europäisches Zusammentreffen
RU	АСЕМ	Азиатско-европейская встреча
		Совещание глав государств и правительств стран
		ЕС и АСЕАН

22

EN	ASEUR	European non-governmental organizations
FR	ASEUR	organisations non-gouvernementales européennes
DE	-	Europäischen Nichtregierungsorganisationen
RU	-	европейские неправительственные организации

23

EN	ASSUC	Association of Professional Organizations of the Sugar Trade for EEC Countries
FR	ASSUC	Association des organisations professionnelles du commerce des sucres pour les pays de la CEE
DE	-	Verband der Berufsorganisationen der EWG-Länder für Zuckerhandel

RU	-	Ассоциация профессиональных организаций стран ЭЭС по торговле сахаром

24

EN	AUA	agricultural unit of account
FR	UCA	unité de compte agricole
DE	LRE	agrarrechnungseinheit
RU	-	сельскохозяйственная расчетная единица

расчетная единица, применявшаяся в 70-е годы в рамках общей сельскохозяйственной политики ЕС;"зеленая" расчетная единица

25

EN	BCC	Business Co-operation Centre
FR	BRE	Bureau de rapprochement des entreprises
DE	BRE	Büro für Unternehmenskooperation
RU	-	Центр делового сотрудничества

оказывает содействие предприятиям ЕС в поиске деловых партнеров

26

EN	BC-NET	Business Co-operation Network
FR	BC-NET	Réseau pour la coopération interentreprises
DE	BC -NET	Netz für Unternehmenskooperation
RU	-	Сеть делового сотрудничества

компьютеризированная система информации о деловом сотрудничестве в ЕС

27

EN	BENELUX	Benelux Economic Union
FR	BENELUX	Union économique Bénélux
DE	BENELUX	Benelux-Wirtschaftsunion
RU	БЕНИЛЮКС	Экономический союз Бельгии, Нидерландов и Люксембурга

28

EN	BEUC	European Bureau of Consumers' Unions
FR	BEUC	Bureau européen des unions de consommateurs
DE	BEUC	Europäisches Büro der Verbraucherverbände
RU	-	Европейское бюро потребительских союзов

объединение союзов потребителей стран ЕС

29

EN	BIC	Community measure for the creation and development of business and innovation centres and their network
FR	BIC	Action communautaire pour la création et le développement de centres ïentreprise et innovation ainsi que de leur réseau

| DE | BIC | Gemeinschaftsaktion zur Schaffung von Unternehmens- und Innovationszentren und zum Aufbau ihrer Netzorganisation |
| RU | - | Меры Сообщества по созданию и развитию сети деловых и инновационных центров |

30

EN	BIOMED	Specific Research and Technological Development Programme in the field of Biomedicine and Health
FR	BIOMED	Programme spécifique de recherche et de développement technologique dans le domaine de la biomédecine et de la santé
DE	BIOMED	Spezifisches Programm für Forschung und technologische Entwicklung im Bereich Biomedizin und Gesundheitswesen
RU	БИОМЕД	Специальная научно-техническая программа в области биомедицины и здравоохранения ЕС

31

EN	BIOTECH	Specific Research and Technological Development Programme in the field of Biotechnology
FR	BIOTECH	Programme spécifique de recherche et de développement technologique dans le domaine de la biotechnologie
DE	BIOTECH	Spezifisches Programm für Forschung und technologische Entwicklung im Bereich der Biotechnologie
RU	БИОТЕК	Специальная научно-техническая программа в области биотехнологии *ЕС*

32

EN	BIS	Bank for International Settlements
FR	BRI	Banque des règlements internationaux
DE	BIZ	Bank für internationalen Zahlungsausgleich
RU	БМР	Банк международных расчетов

33

EN	BLEU	Belgo-Luxembourg Economic Union
FR	UEBL	Union économique belgo-luxembourgeoise
DE	BLWU	Belgisch-luxemburgische Wirtschaftsunion
RU	БЛЭС	Бельго-люксембургский экономический союз

34

EN	BRIDGE	Biotechnology Research for Innovation, Development and Growth in Europe
FR	BRIDGE	Recherches biotechnologiques pour l'innovation, le développement et la croissance en Europe
DE	BRIDGE	Biotechnologieforschung im Dienste von Innovation, Entwicklung und Wachstum in Europa

RU   БРИДЖ   Исследования в области биотехнологии для
                     инновационной деятельности и развития в Европе
                     программа ЕС

35
EN   BRITE   Basic Research in Industrial Technologies in Europe;
                     Multiannual Research and Development Programme of
                     the European Economic Community in the field of
                     Basic Technological Research and the Application of
                     New Technologies
FR   BRITE   Recherche fondamentale dans le domaine des
                     technologies industrielles en Europe; Programme
                     pluriannuel de recherche et de développement pour la
                     Communauté économique européenne dans le domaine
                     de la recherche technologique fondamentale et de
                     l'application des technologies nouvelles
DE   BRITE   Mehrjahresforschungs- und -entwicklungsprogramm
                     der Europäischen Wirtschaftsgemeinschaft auf dem
                     Gebiet der technologischen Grundlagenforschung und
                     der Anwendung neuer Technologien
RU   БРАЙТ   Базисные исследования по проблемам
                     промышленных технологий в Европе;
                     Долгосрочная научно-техническая программа ЕЭС
                     в области базисных исследований и применения
                     новых технологий

36
EN   BRITE/EURAM   Specific Research and Technological Development
                     Programme in the field of Industrial Manufacturing
                     Technologies and Advanced Materials Applications
FR   BRITE/EURAM   Programme spécifique de recherche et de
                     développement technologique de la Communauté
                     économique européenne dans les domaines des
                     technologies industrielles manufacturières et des
                     applications des matériaux avancés
DE   BRITE/EURAM   Wissenschaftstechnisches EWG Spezialprogramm auf
                     dem Gebiete der industriellen Technologie und
                     Verwendung neuer Materialien
RU   БРАЙТ/ЕВРАМ   Специальная научно-техническая программа ЕЭС
                     в области промышленных технологий и
                     применения новых видов материалов

37
EN   BSE   Bovine Spongiform Encephalopathy (mad cow disease)
FR   ESB   encephalopathie spongiforme bovine (maladie de la
                     vache folle)
DE   BSE   Spongiforme Rinderencephalophathie
RU   ВБЭ   вирус бычьего энцефалита ("коровье бешенство")

38
EN	**BTN**	**Brussels Nomenclature**
FR	**NDB**	**Nomenclature de Bruxelles**
DE	**BZT**	**Brüsseler Zolltarifschema**
RU	**БТН**	**Брюссельская таможенная номенклатура**

39
EN	**CA**	**compensatory amounts**
FR	**MC**	**montants compensatoires**
DE	**-**	**Ausgleichsbeträge**
RU	**-**	**компенсационные суммы**

40
EN	**CACM**	**Central American Common Market**
FR	**MCCA**	**Marché commun centraméricain**
DE	**MCCA; MCC**	**Zentralamerikanischer Gemeinsamer Markt**
RU	**ЦАОР**	Центральноамериканский общий рынок

41
EN	**CAIS**	**Central American Integration System**
FR	**SICA**	**Système d'integration centraméricaine**
DE	**-**	**Zentralamerikanisches Integrationssystem**
RU	**ЦСИ**	**Центральноамериканская система интеграции**

42
EN	**CAP**	**Common Agricultural Policy**
FR	**PAC**	**politique agricole commune**
DE	**GAP**	**gemeinsame Agrarpolitik**
RU	**ОСП**	**общая сельскохозяйственная политика** *ЕС*

43
EN	**CBR; BCR**	**Community Bureau of References**
FR	**BCR**	**Bureau communautaire de référence**
DE	**BCR**	**Referenzbüro der Gemeinschaft**
RU	**-**	**Бюро Сообщества по эталонам**
		обеспечивает сопоставимость результатов анализов и измерений в странах ЕС

44
EN	**CBSS**	**Council of the Baltic Sea States**
FR	**CEMB**	**Conseil des Etats de la Mer Baltique**
DE	**-**	**Ostseestaatenrat**
RU	**-**	**Совет государств Балтийского моря**

45
EN	**CBT**	**cross-border trade**
FR	**-**	**commerce transfrontalier**
DE	**CBT**	**grenzüberschreitender Verkehr**
RU	**-**	**трансграничная торговля**

46

EN	CCAM	Advisory Committee on Procurements and Contracts
FR	CCAM	Commission consultative des achats et des marchés
DE	CCAM	Vergabebeirat
RU	-	Консультативный комитет по закупкам и контрактам

47

EN	CCC	Customs Co-operation Council
FR	CCD	Conseil de coopération douanière
DE	RZZ; BZR	Rat für die Zusammenarbeit auf dem Gebiete des Zollwesens; Brüsseler Zollrat
RU	CTC	Совет таможенного сотрудничества (*в настоящее время Всемирная таможенная организация*)

48

EN	CCCC	Community-COST Concertation Committee
FR	CCCC	Comité de concertation Communauté-COST
DE	-	Auschuss für Vereinbarung der Gemeinschaft-COST
RU	-	Комитет по согласованию Сообщество-КОСТ

49

EN	CCEE	countries of Central and Eastern Europe
FR	PECO	pays ïEurope centrale et orientale
DE	MOEL	mittel- und osteuropäische Länder
RU	-	страны Центральной и Восточной Европы

50

EN	CCEET	Centre for Co-operation with European Economies in Transition
FR	CCEET	Centre pour la coopération avec les économies européennes en transition
DE	-	Zusammenarbeitszentrum für europäischen Länder im wirtschaftlichen Umbruch
RU	-	Центр сотрудничества с европейскими странами с переходной экономикой ОЭСР

51

EN	CCFF	compensatory and contingency financing facility
FR	FFCFI	facilité de financement compensatoire et de financement pour imprévus
DE	CCFF	Sonderfazilität zur Kompensations- und Eventualfinanzierung
RU	-	компенсационное финансирование и кредиты на непредвиденные расходы

52

EN	CCG	Policy Co-ordination Group for Credit Insurance, Credit Guarantees and Financial Credits
FR	CCG	groupe de coordination des politiques ïassurance-crédit, des garanties et des crédits financiers
DE	-	Arbeitskreis zur Koordinierung der Politik auf dem Gebiet der Kreditversicherung, der Bürgschaften und der Finanzkredite
RU	-	Группа по координации политики в области страхования кредитов, гарантий и финансовых кредитов *ОЭСР*

53

EN	CCNR	Central Commission for the Navigation of the Rhine
FR	CCNR	Commission centrale pour la navigation du Rhin
DE	ZKR	Zentralkommission für die Rheinschiffahrt
RU	ЦКСР	Центральная комиссия судоходства на Рейне

54

EN	CCT	Common Customs Tariff
FR	TDC	tarif douanier commun
DE	GZT	gemeinsamer Zolltarif
RU	OTT; ETT	общий таможенный тариф; единый таможенный тариф *ЕС*

55

EN	CDH	European Court of Human Rights
FR	CDH	Cour européenne des droits de l'homme
DE	CDH	Konferenz für die menschliche Dimension
RU	-	Европейский суд по правам человека *орган Совета Европы*

56

EN	CDIC	Commission's Steering Committee for Data Processing
FR	CDIC	Comité directeur de l'informatique de la Commission
DE	CDIC	Lenkungsausschuss für Informatik bei der Kommission
RU	-	Комитет по правилам обработки информации при Европейской комиссии

57

EN	CE	compulsory expenditure
FR	DO	dépenses obligatoires
DE	OA	obligatorische Ausgaben
RU	-	обязательные расходы *(в бюджете ЕС)*

58

EN	CE	Council of Europe
FR	CE	Conseil de l'Europe
DE	-	Europarat
RU	CE	Совет Европы
		европейская межправительственная организация

59

EN	CEA	Confederation of European Agriculture
FR	CEA	Confédération européenne de l'agriculture
DE	CEA	Verband der europäischen Landwirtschaft
RU	-	Европейская конфедерация сельского хозяйства
		профессиональная организация в ЕС

60

EN	CECD	European Confederation for Retail Trade
FR	CECD	Confédération européenne du commerce de détail
DE	CECD	Verband des europäischen Einzelhandels
RU	-	Европейская конфедерация розничной торговли
		профессиональная организация в ЕС

61

EN	CECIMO	European Committee for Co-operation of the Machine Tool Industries
FR	CECIMO	Comité européen de coopération des industries de la machine-outil
DE	CECIMO	Europäisches Komitee für die Zusammenarbeit der Werkzeugmaschinenindustrien
RU	СЕСИМО	Европейский комитет по сотрудничеству отраслей станкостроительной промышленности
		профессиональная организация в ЕС

62

EN	CECODE	European Centre for Retail Trade
FR	CECODE	Centre européen du commerce de détail
DE	CECODE	Zentrum des europäischen Einzelhandels
RU	ЕЦРТ	Европейский центр розничной торговли
		профессиональная организация в ЕС

63

EN	CEDEFOP	European Centre for the Development of Vocational Training
FR	CEDEFOP	Centre européen pour le développement de la formation professionnelle
DE	CEDEFOP	Europäisches Zentrum für die Förderung der Berufsbildung
RU	-	Европейский центр по развитию профессионального обучения *ЕС*

64

EN	CEE	Central and Eastern Europe
FR	ECO	Europe centrale et orientale
DE	-	Zentral- und Osteuropa
RU	ЦВЕ	Центральная и Восточная Европа

65

EN	CEEP	European Centre for Public Enterprises
FR	CEEP	Centre européen de l'entreprise publique
DE	CEEP	Europäischer Zentralverband der öffentlichen Wirtschaft
RU	-	Европейский центр государственных предприятий *профессиональная организация в ЕС*

66

EN	CEFTA	Central European Free Trade Agreement
FR	CEFTA	Zone de libre-échange en Europe centrale
DE	-	Zentraleuropäisches Freihandelsabkommen
RU	ЦЕФТА;ЦЕССТ	Центральноевропейское соглашение о свободной торговле

67

EN	CELEX	Interinstitutional Computerized Documentation System for Community Law
FR	CELEX	Système interinstitutionnel de documentation automatisée pour le droit communautaire
DE	CELEX	Interinstitutionelles System für die automatisierte Dokumentation des Gemeinschaftsrechts
RU	СЕЛЕКС	Межинституциональная компьютеризированная система документации по праву Сообщества

68

EN	CEN, ECS	European Committee for Standardization
FR	CEN	Comité européen de normalisation
DE	CEN	Europäisches Komitee für Normung
RU	СЕН	Европейский комитет по стандартизации

69

EN	CENELEC	European Committee for Electrotechnical Standardization
FR	CENELEC	Comité européen de normalisation électrotechnique
DE	CENELEC	Europäisches Komitee für elektrotechnische Normung
RU	СЕНЭЛЕК	Европейский комитет по стандартизации в электротехнике

70

EN	CEPS	Centre for European Policy Studies

FR	CEPS	Centre d'études de la politique européenne
DE	CEPS	Zentrum für europäische politische Forschungen
RU	-	Центр европейских политических исследований

71

EN	CEPT	European Conference of Postal and Telecommunications Administrations
FR	CEPT	Conférence européenne des administrations des postes et des télécommunications
DE	CEPT	Europäische Konferenz der Verwaltungen für Post und Fernmeldewesen
RU	СЕПТ	Европейская конференция почтовой и телефонно-телеграфной связи

72

EN	CERN	European Organization for Nuclear Research
FR	CERN	Organisation européenne pour la recherche nucléaire
DE	CERN	Europäische Organisation für Kernforschung
RU	ЦЕРН	Европейская организация ядерных исследований

73

EN	CESIS	European Centre of the Schengen Information System
FR	CESIS	Centre européen du Système d'information Schengen
DE	-	Europäisches Zentrum des Schengeninformationssystems
RU	-	Европейский центр Шенгенской информационной системы *EC*

74

EN	CET	Common External Tariff
FR	TEC	tarif extérieur commun
DE	GAZ	Gemeinsamer äußerer Zolltarif
RU	-	общий внешний (таможенный) тариф *EC*

75

EN	CETIS	European Scientific Data-processing Centre
FR	CETIS	Centre européen de traitement de l'information scientifique
DE	CETIS	Europäische Zentralstelle für die Verarbeitung wissenschaftlicher Informationen
RU	-	Европейский центр обработки научной информации

76

EN	CEVNI	European Code for Inland Waterways

FR	CEVNI	Code européen des voies de navigation intérieure
DE	-	Europäisches Gesetzbuch für die Schifffahrt auf Binnenwasserstrassen
RU	-	Европейский кодекс судоходства по внутренним водным путям

77

EN	CFF	compensatory financing facility
FR	FFC; CFF	facilité de financement compensatoire
DE	CFF	Möglichkeit der Ausgleichsfinanzierung
RU	-	компенсационное финансирование

78

EN	CFI	Court of First Instance
FR	TPI	Tribunal de première instance
DE	-	Gericht erster Instanz
RU	-	Суд первой инстанции
		EC

79

EN	CFP	Common Fisheries Policy
FR	PCP	politique commune de la pêche
DE	-	gemeinsame Fischereipolitik
RU	-	общая рыболовная политика
		EC

80

EN	CFSP	Common Foreign and Security Policy
FR	PESC	politique étrangère et de sécurité commune
DE	GASP	Gemeinsame Aussen- und Sicherheitspolitik
RU	-	общая внешняя политика и политика безопасности
		EC

81

EN	CIC	Committee on Industrial Co-operation
FR	CCI	Comité de coopération industrielle
DE	AIZ	Ausschuss für industrielle Zusammenarbeit
RU	-	Комитет по промышленному сотрудничеству
		предусмотрен Ломейскими конвенциями между ЕС и странами АКТ

82

EN	CIEAR; IEAR	European Communities Institute for Economic Analysis and Research
FR	ICARE; IARE	Institut des Communautés européennes pour l'analyse et la recherche économiques
DE	ICARE; IARE	Institut der Europäischen Gemeinschaften für Wirtschaftsanalyse und - forschung

RU	-	Институт экономического анализа и исследований Европейских сообществ

83

EN	CIRCE	European Communities Information and Documentary Research Centre
FR	CIRCE	Centre d'information et de recherche documentaire des Communautés européennes
DE	CIRCE	Informations- und Dokumentationszentrale der Europäischen Gemeinschaften
RU	-	Исследовательский центр в области информации и документации Европейских сообществ

84

EN	CIS	Commonwealth of Independent States
FR	CEI	Communauté des Etats indépendants
DE	GUS	Gemeinschaft Unabhängiger Staaten
RU	СНГ	Содружество независимых государств

85

EN	CIS	Customs Information System
FR	SID	Système d'information douanier
DE	ZIS; SID	Zollinformationssystem
RU	-	Система таможенной информации

86

EN	CISSP	Community Information System on Social Protection
FR	CISSP	Système d'information mutuelle sur la protection sociale dans la Communauté
DE	CISSP	System zur gegenseitigen Information über den sozialen Schutz in der Gemeinschaft
RU	-	Информационная система Сообщества по социальной защите

87

EN	CJEC	Court of Justice of the European Communities
FR	CJCE	Cour de justice des Communautés européennes
DE	EuGH	Gerichtshof der Europäischen Gemeinschaften
RU	-	Суд Европейских сообществ

88

EN	CJUS	law database (judgements of the Court of Justice)
FR	CJUS	banque de données juridiques (arrêts de la Cour de justice)
DE	CJUS	Juristische Datenbasis (Urteile des Gerichtshofs)
RU	-	банк данных о решениях Суда ЕС

89

EN	CLIO	Code of Liberalization of Current Invisible Operations

FR	CLIO	Code de libération des opérations invisibles courantes
DE	-	Gesetzbuch für Lieberalisierung der laufenden unsichtbaren Transaktionen
RU	-	Кодекс либерализации текущих невидимых операций *ОЭСР*

90

EN	CMEA;COMECON	Council for Mutual Economic Assistance
FR	CAEM;COMECON	Conseil d'assistance économique mutuelle
DE	RGW;COMECON	Rat für gegenseitige Wirtschaftshilfe
RU	СЭВ	Совет экономической взаимопомощи

91

EN	CMIT	Committee on Capital Movements and Invisible Transactions
FR	CMIT	Comité des mouvements de capitaux et des transactions invisibles
DE	CMIT	Ausschuss für Kapitalverkehr und unsichtbare Transaktionen
RU	КМИТ	Комитет по движению капиталов и невидимым операциям *ОЭСР*

92

EN	COCOM	Co-ordinating Committee on Export Controls
FR	COCOM	Comité de coordination pour le contrôle multilatéral des exportations
DE	COCOM	Koordinierungskomitee für die multilaterale Exportkontrolle
RU	КОКОМ	Координационный комитет по контролю над экспортом *(в бывшие социалистические страны; ликвидирован в 1994 г.)*

93

EN	CODEST	Committee for the European Development of Science and Technology
FR	CODEST	Comité de développement européen de la science et de la technologie
DE	CODEST	Komitee für die Entwicklung der europäischen Wissenschaft und Technologie
RU	КОДЕСТ	Комитет по развитию европейской науки и технологии *ЕС*

94

EN	COFACE	Confederation of Family Organizations in the European Community
FR	COFACE	Confédération des organisations familiales de la Communauté européenne
DE	COFACE	Bund der Familienorganisationen der Europäischen Gemeinschaft
RU	-	Конфедерация семейных организаций Европейского сообщества

95

EN	COGECA	General Committee for Agricultural Co-operation in the European Community
FR	COGECA	Comité général de la coopération agricole de la Communauté européenne
DE	COGECA	Allgemeiner Ausschuss des ländlichen Genossenschaftswesens der Europäischen Gemeinschaft
RU	-	Генеральный комитет по сельскохозяйственному сотрудничеству в Европейском сообществе *профессиональная организация*

96

EN	COM	Common organization of the markets
FR	OCM	organisation commune de marché
DE	GMO	Gemeinsame Marktorganisation
RU	-	общая организация рынков *сельскохозяйственная политика ЕС*

97

EN	COMEL	Co-ordinating Committee for Common Market Associations of Manufacturers of Rotating Electrical Machinery
FR	COMEL	Comité de coordination des constructeurs de machines tournantes électriques du Marché commun
DE	COMEL	EWG-Zusammenarbeit der Fachverbände der Hersteller von elektrischen Maschinen
RU	-	Координационный комитет ассоциаций производителей вращающихся электрических машин стран Общего рынка *профессиональная организация в ЕС*

98

EN	COMETT	Community Programme for Education and Training for Technologies; Programme on Co-operation between Universities and Industry regarding Training in the field of Technology
FR	COMETT	Programme de coopération entre l'université et l'entreprise en matière de formation dans le cadre des technologies

DE	COMETT	Programm zur Zusammenarbeit von Hochschule und Unternehmen hinsichtlich der Ausbildung auf dem Gebiet der Technologie
RU	КОМЕТТ	Программа Сообщества в целях образования и профессионального обучения в области технологии; Программа сотрудничества между университетами и промышленностью в подготовке специалистов в области технологии

99

EN	COMITEXTIL	Co-ordinating Committee for the Textile Industries in the EC
FR	COMITEXTIL	Comité de coordination des industries textiles de la CE
DE	COMITEXTIL	Koordinierungskomitee der Textilindustrien der EG
RU	-	Координационный комитет текстильной промышленности ЕС *профессиональная организация*

100

EN	COPA	Committee of Agricultural Organizations in the European Community
FR	COPA	Comité des organisations professionnelles agricoles de la Communauté européenne
DE	COPA	Ausschuss der berufsständischen landwirtschaftlichen Organisationen der Europäischen Gemeinschaft
RU	-	Комитет сельскохозяйственных организаций Европейского сообщества *профессиональная организация*

101

EN	COPENUR	Standing Committee on Uranium Enrichment
FR	COPENUR	Comité permanent pour l'enrichissement de l'uranium
DE	COPENUR	Ständiger Ausschuss für Urananreicherung
RU	-	Постоянный комитет по обогащению урана *ЕС*

102

EN	COPMEC	Committee of Small and Medium-sized Commercial Enterprises of the EC Countries
FR	COPMEC	Comité des petites et moyennes entreprises commerciales des pays de la CE
DE	COPMEC	Komitee der Klein- und Mittelbetriebe des Handels der EG-Länder
RU	-	Комитет по малым и средним торговым предприятиям стран ЕС

103
EN	CoR	Committee of the Regions
FR	CdR	Comité des Régions
DE	AdR	Ausschuss der Regionen
RU	-	Комитет регионов
		ЕС

104
EN	CORDIS	Community Research and Development Information Service
FR	CORDIS	Service d'information sur la recherche et le développement communautaires
DE	CORDIS	Informationsdienst der Gemeinschaft für Forschung und Entwicklung
RU	КОРДИС	Служба информации о деятельности Сообщества в сфере НИОКР
		программа ЕС

105
EN	COREPER; PRC	Permanent Representatives Committee
FR	COREPER; CRP	Comité des représentants permanents
DE	AStV	Ausschuss der Ständigen Vertreter
RU	КОРЕПЕР	Комитет постоянных представителей
		(государств-членов ЕС)

106
EN	CORINE	Co-ordination of Information on the Environment; Commission work programme concerning an experimental project for gathering, co-ordinating and ensuring the consistency of information on the state of the environment and natural resources in the Community
FR	CORINE	Programme de travail de la Commission concernant un projet expérimental pour la collecte, la coordination et la mise en cohérence de l'information sur l'état de l'environnement et des ressources naturelles dans la Communauté
DE	CORINE	Arbeitsprogramm der Kommission für ein Versuchsvorhaben für die Zusammenstellung, Koordinierung und Abstimmung der Informationen über den Zustand der Umwelt und der natürlichen Ressourcen in der Gemeinschaft
RU	-	Координация информации по окружающей среде; Рабочая программа Комиссии, касающаяся сбора, координации и обеспечения сопоставимости информации о состоянии окружающей среды и природных ресурсах в Сообществе

107

EN	COS 113	Article 113 Committee
FR	COS 113	Comité spécial de l'article 113
DE	COS 113	Besonderer Ausschuss Artikel 113
RU	-	Комитет по статье 113
		(Договора о ЕЭС)

108

EN	COSAC	Conference of bodies concerned with Community affairs in the Parliaments of the European Community
FR	COSAC	Conférence des organes spécialisés dans les affaires communautaires des parlements de la Communauté européenne
DE	-	Konferenz der Organe beschäftigt mit der Tätigkeit der EU in den Parlamenten der EG-Länder
RU	-	Конференция органов, занимающихся вопросами деятельности ЕС в парламентах стран Европейского сообщества

109

EN	COST	European Co-operation in the field of Scientific and Technical Research
FR	COST	Coopération européenne dans le domaine de la recherche scientifique et technique
DE	COST	Europäische Zusammenarbeit auf dem Gebiet der wissenschaftlichen und technischen Forschung
RU	КОСТ	Европейское научно-техническое сотрудничество

110

EN	COTACEX	Technical Committee of Export Credit Insurers of the EC
FR	COTACEX	Comité technique des assureurs-crédit à l'exportation de la CE
DE	COTACEX	Fachausschuss der Ausfuhr-Kreditversicherer der EG
RU	-	Технический комитет страхователей экспортных кредитов ЕС

111

EN	CP	contracting party
FR	PC	partie contractante
DE	-	Vertragspartei
RU	-	договаривающаяся сторона

112

EN	CPC	Community Patent Convention; Convention for the European Patent for the Common Market
FR	CBC	Convention sur le brevet communautaire; Convention relative au brevet européen pour le Marché commun

| DE | GPÜ | Gemeinschaftspatentübereinkommen; Übereinkommen über das europäische Patent für den Gemeinsamen Markt |
| RU | - | Конвенция о патенте Сообщества; Конвенция о европейском патенте для Общего рынка |

113

EN	CPEMT	Medium-term Economic Policy Committee
FR	CPEMT	Comité de politique économique à moyen terme
DE	CPEMT	Ausschuss für mittelfristige Wirtschaftspolitik
RU	-	Комитет по среднесрочной экономической политике *ЕС*

114

EN	CPR	Regional Policy Committee
FR	CPR	Comité de politique régionale
DE	CPR	Ausschuss für Regionalpolitik
RU	-	Комитет по региональной политике *ЕС*

115

EN	CREST	Scientific and Technical Research Committee
FR	CREST	Comité de la recherche scientifique et technique
DE	CREST; AWTF	Ausschuss für wissenschaftliche und technische Forschung
RU	КРЕСТ	Комитет по научным и техническим исследованиям *ЕС*

116

EN	CRONOS	Database of the Statistical Office of the European Communities for the Management of Time Series
FR	CRONOS	base de données de l'Office statistique des Communautés européennes pour la gestion de séries chronologiques
DE	CRONOS	Zeitreihendatenbank des Statistischen Amtes der Europäischen Gemeinschaften
RU	-	банк данных Статистического бюро Европейских сообществ по ведению динамических рядов

117

EN	CSCE	Conference on Security and Co-operation in Europe
FR	CSCE	Conférence sur la sécurité et la coopération en Europe
DE	KSZE	Konferenz über Sicherheit und Zusammenarbeit in Europa
RU	СБСЕ	Конференция по безопасности и сотрудничеству в Европе

118

| EN | CSCM | Conference for Security and Co-operation in the Mediterranean |

FR	CSCM	Conférence sur la sécurité et la coopération en Méditerrannée
DE	-	Konferenz für Sicherheit und Zusammenarbeit in Mittelmeerländern
RU	-	Конференция по безопасности и сотрудничеству в Средиземноморье

119

EN	CSF	Community support framework
FR	CCA	cadre communautaire d'appui
DE	DPP/GFK	Programmplanungsdokument (Strukturfonds), Gemeinschaftliches Förderkonzept
RU	-	система поддержки Сообщества *структурные фонды ЕС*

120

EN	CSTP	Committee for Scientific and Technological Policy
FR	CPST	Comité de la politique scientifique et technologique
DE	CSTP	Ausschuss für Wissenschaftspolitik und Technologiepolitik
RU	-	Комитет по научно-технической политике *ЕС*

121

EN	CTIC	Trans-border Information and Consulting Centres for Consumers
FR	CTIC	centres transfrontaliers d'information et de conseil des consommateurs
DE	CTIC	Grenzübergreifende Informations- und Beratungszentren für Verbraucher
RU	-	центры информации и консультаций для потребителей о трансграничной торговле *ЕС*

122

EN	CTR's	common technical regulations
FR	RTC	réglementations techniques communes
DE	CTRs	gemeinsame technische Vorschriften
RU	-	общие технические правила *общие обязательные требования к продукции в ЕС*

123

EN	CTS	conformance-testing services
FR	CTS	services d'essais de conformité
DE	-	Übereinstimmungkontrollen der Produktion
RU	-	службы по проверке соответствия продукции *(техническим требованиям ЕС)*

124

| EN | DAC | Development Assistance Committee |

FR	CAD	Comité de l'aide au développement
DE	DAC	Ausschuss für Entwicklungshilfe
RU	-	Комитет помощи развитию
		ОЭСР

125
EN	DEP	European Depositary Library
FR	DEP	Bibliothèque dépositaire européenne
DE	EDB	Europäische Depositarbibliothek
RU	-	Европейская депозитарная библиотека *ЕС*

126
EN	DG	Directorate-General
FR	DG	direction générale
DE	GD	Generaldirektion
RU	-	генеральный директорат
		подразделение в аппарате Европейской Комиссии и
		других органов ЕС

127
EN	DIANE	Direct Information Access Network for Europe
FR	DIANE	Réseau d'accès direct à l'information pour l'Europe
DE	DIANE	Informationsnetz mit Direktzugriff für Europa
RU	ДИАНЕ	Европейская сеть прямого доступа к информации
		ЕС

128
EN	DOSES	Development of statistical expert systems
FR	DOSES	Développement des systèmes experts en statistiques
DE	DOSES	Entwicklung der Sachverständigen Systeme in Statistik
RU	ДОЗЕС	Развитие экспертных систем в статистике
		программа ЕС по использованию передовой
		технологии в обработке статистических данных

129
EN	DRIVE	Dedicated Road Infrastructure for Vehicle Safety in Europe; Community Programme in the field of Road Transport Informatics and Telecommunications
FR	DRIVE	Programme communautaire dans le domaine de l'informatique du transport routier et des télécommunications
DE	DRIVE	Gemeinschaftsprogramm auf dem Gebiet der Strassenverkehrsinformatik und -telekommunikation
RU	ДРАЙВ	Специальная дорожная инфраструктура в целях безопасности автотранспорта в Европе; Программа Сообщества в области информационной технологии и телекоммуникаций в автодорожном транспорте

130

EN	**EA**	European association
FR	**AE**	association européenne
DE	-	Europäische Assoziation
RU	-	европейская ассоциация

форма сотрудничества компаний нескольких стран ЕС

131

EN	**EAC**	European Agency for Co-operation
FR	**AEC**	Agence européenne de coopération
DE	**EAZ**	Europäische Agentur für Zusammenarbeit
RU	-	Европейское агентство по сотрудничеству

132

EN	**EAD**	Euro-Arab Dialogue
FR	**DEA**	dialogue euro-arabe
DE	-	Europäisch-arabischer Dialog
RU	-	евроарабский диалог

переговоры ЕС со странами-членами Лиги арабских государств

133

EN	**EAEC;EURATOM**	European Atomic Energy Community
FR	**CEEA;EURATOM**	Communauté européenne de l'énergie atomique
DE	**EAG;EURATOM**	Europäische Atomgemeinschaft
RU	**ЕВРАТОМ**	Европейское сообщество по атомной энергии

134

EN	**EAGGF**	European Agricultural Guidance and Guarantee Fund
FR	**FEOGA**	Fonds européen d'orientation et de garantie agricole
DE	**EAGFL**	Europäischer Ausrichtungs- und Garantiefonds für die Landwirtschaft
RU	**ЕФОГ; ФЕОГА**	Европейский фонд ориентации и гарантии сельского хозяйства; Сельскохозяйственный фонд

фонд для финансирования общей сельскохозяйственной политики ЕС

135

EN	**EAMA**	European Automobile Manufacturers' Association
FR	**ACEA**	Association des constructeurs européens d'automobiles
DE	-	Vereinigung der europäischen Autohersteller
RU	-	Ассоциация европейских производителей автомобилей

профессиональная организация в ЕС

136
EN	**EAPN**	**European anti-poverty network**
FR	**EAPN**	**réseau européen des associations de lutte contre la pauvrété et l'exclusion sociale**
DE	-	**Europäisches Netz von der Assoziationen gegen Armut**
RU	-	**Европейская сеть ассоциаций по борьбе с бедностью**

объединение организаций стран-членов ЕС

137
EN	**EBA**	**ECU Banking Association**
FR	-	**Association bancaire pour l'ecu**
DE	-	**ECU Bankassoziation**
RU	-	**Банковская ассоциация ЭКЮ**

ассоциация банков, специализирующихся на операциях в ЭКЮ

138
EN	**EBC**	**European Business Council**
FR	**EBC**	**Conseil des affaires européennes**
DE	-	**Europäischer Businessrat**
RU	-	**Совет европейского бизнеса**

орган, представляющий интересы предприятий ЕС в Японии

139
EN	**EBRD**	**European Bank for Reconstruction and Development**
FR	**BERD**	**Banque européenne pour la reconstruction et le développement**
DE	**EBWE**	**Europäische Bank für Wiederaufbau und Entwicklung**
RU	**ЕБРР**	**Европейский банк реконструкции и развития**

140
EN	**EC**	**European Community**
FR	**CE**	**Communauté européenne**
DE	**EG**	**Europäische Gemeinschaft**
RU	**ЕС**	**Европейское сообщество**

141
EN	**ECAC**	**European Civil Aviation Conference**
FR	**CEAC**	**Commission européenne de l'aviation civile**
DE	**ECAC**	**Europäische Zivilluftfahrtkonferenz**
RU	**ЕКАК**	**Европейская конференция гражданской авиации**

142
EN	**ECAS**	**Euro Citizen Action Service**
FR	**ECAS**	**Euro citoyen action et service**

DE	-	Europa Bürger Konsultationsdienst
RU	-	Консультационная служба в рамках программы "Европа граждан"
		ЕС

143

EN	ECB	European Central Bank
FR	BCE	Banque centrale européenne
DE	EZB	Europäische Zentralbank
RU	ЕЦБ	Европейский центральный банк
		предусмотрен Договором о Европейском Союзе

144

EN	ECCO	European Communities Communications Office
FR	ECCO	Bureau de communication des Communautés européennes
DE	-	Verbindungsbüro der Europäischen Gemeinschaften
RU	-	Бюро по связям Европейских сообществ

145

EN	ECE; UNECE	(United Nations) Economic Commission for Europe
FR	CEE	Commission économique (des Nations unies) pour l'Europe
DE	ECE	Wirtschaftskommission für Europa (der Vereinten Nationen)
RU	ЭЭК	Европейская экономическая комиссия (ООН)

146

EN	ECET	European country in economic transition
FR	-	pays européen en cours de mutation économique
DE	ECET	europäische Länder im wirtschaftlichen Umbruch
RU	-	европейская страна с переходной экономикой

147

EN	ECF	European Cultural Foundation
FR	FEC	Fondation européenne de la culture
DE	ECF	Europäischer Kulturfonds
RU	-	Европейский культурный фонд
		ЕС

148

EN	ECHO	European Community Humanitarian Office
FR	ECHO	Office humanitaire de la Communauté européenne
DE	ECHO	Amt der Europäischen Gemeinschaft für humanitäre Hilfe
RU	-	Бюро Европейского сообщества по гуманитарной помощи

149

EN	ECI	Euratom classified information
FR	CSE	connaissances secrètes de l'Euratom
DE	EVS	Euratom-Verschlusssachen
RU	-	конфиденциальная информация Евратома

150

EN	ECIP; ECIIP	European Community International Investment Partners
FR	ECIP	Partenaires internationaux de la Communauté européenne dans le domaine d'investissements
DE	ECIP	Internationale Investitionspartner der Europäischen Gemeinschaft
RU	-	Международные партнеры Европейского сообщества в области инвестиций *финансовый инструмент поддержки инвестиций частных предприятий ЕС в странах Средиземноморья, Латинской Америки и Азии*

151

EN	ECITU	European Confederation of Independent Trade Unions
FR	CESI	Confédération européenne des syndicats indépendants
DE	-	Europäischer Bund der Unabhängigen Gewerkschaften
RU	-	Европейская конфедерация независимых профсоюзов *ЕС*

152

EN	ECLAIR	European collaborative linkage of agriculture and industry through research. Multiannual programme for biotechnology-based agro-industrial research and technology development.
FR	ECLAIR	Programme pluriannuel de recherche et de développement technologique dans le domaine agro-industriel, basé sur les biotechnologies
DE	ECLAIR	Mehrjähriges Programm für biotechnologische, agroindustrielle Forschung und technologische Entwicklung
RU	ЭКЛЭР	Европейское сотрудничество сельского хозяйства и промышленности через исследования; Долгосрочная программа ЕС по научно-техническому сотрудничеству в сельском хозяйстве и промышленности на базе достижений биотехнологии

153

EN	**ECMA**	**European Computer Manufacturers' Association**
FR	**ECMA**	**Association européenne des constructeurs d'ordinateurs**
DE	**-**	**Vereinigung der europäischen Computerhersteller**
RU	**-**	**Европейская ассоциация производителей компьютеров**
		профессиональная организация в ЕС

154

EN	**ECMT**	**European Conference of Ministers of Transport**
FR	**CEMT**	**Conférence européenne des ministres des transports**
DE	**CEMT**	**Europäische Konferenz der Verkehrminister**
RU	**ЕКМТ**	**Европейская конференция министров транспорта**

155

EN	**ECO**	**Economic Co-operation Organization**
FR	**ECO**	**Organisation de coopération économique**
DE	**ECO**	**Organisation für wirtschaftliche Zusammenarbeit**
RU	**ОЭС**	**Организация экономического сотрудничества**
		члены ОЭС: Азербайджан, Афганистан, Иран, Казахстан, Киргизия, Пакистан, Таджикистан, Туркменистан, Турция, Узбекистан

156

EN	**ECOFIN**	**ECOFIN Council; EU Council composed by the Ministers of Economy and Finance**
FR	**ECOFIN**	**Conseil ECOFIN; Conseil de l'UE composé des ministres de l'économie et des finances**
DE	**-**	**EU-Rat der Wirtschafts- und Finanzminister**
RU	**ЭКОФИН**	**Совет ЕС в составе министров экономики и финансов**
		(государств-членов)

157

EN	**ECOSOC; ESC; ECSOCO**	**Economic and Social Council**
FR	**ECOSOC**	**Conseil économique et social**
DE	**ECOSOC; WSR**	**Wirtschafts- und Sozialrat**
RU	**ЭКОСОС**	**Экономический и социальный совет**
		ООН

158

EN	**ECS**	**European Communications Satellite**
FR	**ECS**	**satellite de communication européen**
DE	**-**	**Europäischer Fernmeldesatellit**
RU	**-**	**европейский спутник связи**

159

EN	**ECSC**	**European Coal and Steel Community**
FR	**CECA**	**Communauté européenne du charbon et de l'acier**
DE	**EGKS**	**Europäische Gemeinschaft für Kohle und Stahl**
RU	**ЕОУС**	**Европейское объединение угля и стали**

160

EN	**ECTRA**	**European Committee for Telecommunications Regulatory Affaires**
FR	**ECTRA**	**Comité européen pour les questions réglementaires de télécommunications**
DE	**ECTRA**	**Europäischer Ausschuss für Regulierungsfragen des Fernmeldewesens**
RU	-	**Европейский комитет по вопросам регулирования телекоммуникаций**

161

EN	**ECU**	**European Currency Unit**
FR	**ECU**	**unité monétaire européenne**
DE	**ECU**	**Europäische Währungseinheit**
RU	**ЭКЮ**	**европейская валютная единица**

162

EN	**EDC**	**European Defence Community**
FR	**CED**	**Communauté européenne de défense**
DE	**EVG**	**Europäische Verteidigungsgemeinschaft**
RU	-	**Европейское оборонительное сообщество**
		попытка создания предпринималась в 50-е годы

163

EN	**EDC**	**European Documentation Centre**
FR	**CDE**	**Centre de documentation européenne**
DE	**CDE**	**Zentrum für Europäische Dokumentation**
RU	-	**Центр документации ЕС**

164

EN	**EDF**	**European Development Fund**
FR	**FED**	**Fonds européen de développement**
DE	**EEF**	**Europäischer Entwicklungsfonds**
RU	**ЕФР**	**Европейский фонд развития**
		предоставляет помощь ЕС странам АКТ

165

EN	**EDI**	**electronic data interchange; electronic document interchange**
FR	**EDI**	**échange de données informatisé; échange électronique de données**
DE	**EDI**	**elektronischer Datenaustausch**
RU	-	**электронный обмен данными** *ЕС*

166

EN	**EDN**	**Europe of Nations Group (Coordination Group)**
FR	**EDN**	**groupe Europe des Nations (groupe de coordination)**
DE	**EDN**	**Fraktion Europa der Nationen (Koordinierungsgruppe)**
RU	**-**	**группа "Европа наций" (координирующая группа)**
		фракция в Европейском Парламенте

167

EN	**EEA**	**European Economic Area**
FR	**EEE**	**Espace économique européen**
DE	**EWR**	**Europäischer Wirtschaftsraum**
RU	**ЕЭП**	**Европейское экономическое пространство**
		включает страны ЕС и страны ЕАСТ

168

EN	**EEA**	**European Environment Agency**
FR	**AEE**	**Agence européenne pour l'environnement**
DE	**-**	**Europäische Umweltagentur**
RU	**-**	**Европейское агентство по окружающей среде**
		ЕС

169

EN	**EEB**	**European Environmental Bureau**
FR	**BEE**	**Bureau européen de l'environnement**
DE	**EEB**	**Europäisches Umweltbüro**
RU	**-**	**Европейское бюро по окружающей среде**
		объединение экологических организаций стран-членов
		ЕС

170

EN	**EEC**	**European Economic Community**
FR	**CEE**	**Communauté économique européenne**
DE	**EWG**	**Europäische Wirtschaftsgemeinschaft**
RU	**ЕЭС**	**Европейское экономическое сообщество**

171

EN	**EECIF**	**European Export Credit Insurance Facility**
FR	**SEACE**	**Système européen d'assurance-crédit à l'exportation**
DE	**EEKVF**	**Europäische Exportkreditversicherungs-Fazilität**
RU	**-**	**Европейская система страхования экспортных**
		кредитов
		ЕС

172

EN	**EEIG**	**European Economic Interest Grouping**
FR	**GEIE**	**groupement européen d'intérêt économique**
DE	**EWIV**	**Europäische wirtschaftliche Interessenvereinigung**

RU   **ЕОЭИ**   европейское объединение по экономическим
интересам
*форма сотрудничества компаний нескольких стран
ЕС*

173
EN   **EEMIN**   **European Environment Monitoring and Information
Network**
FR   **EEMIN**   **Réseau européen de surveillance et d'information sur
l'environnement**
DE   **-**   **Europäisches Umwelt Überwachungs- und
Informationssystem**
RU   **-**   **Европейская система наблюдения и информации об
окружающей среде**

174
EN   **EFC**   **European Farmers' Co-ordination**
FR   **CPE**   **Coordination paysanne européenne**
DE   **-**   **Europäische Bauern-Koordination**
RU   **-**   **Координация европейских фермеров**
профессиональная организация в ЕС

175
EN   **EFILWC**   **European Foundation for the Improvement of Living
and Working Conditions**
FR   **FEACVT**   **Fondation européenne pour l'amélioration des
conditions de vie et de travail**
DE   **-**   **Europäische Stiftung zur Verbesserung der Lebens-
und Arbeitsbedingungen**
RU   **-**   **Европейский фонд улучшения условий жизни и
работы**
ЕС

176
EN   **EFTA**   **European Free Trade Association**
FR   **AELE**   **Association européenne de libre-échange**
DE   **EFTA**   **Europäische Freihandelsassoziation**
RU   **ЕАСТ**   **Европейская ассоциация свободной торговли**

177
EN   **EIB**   **European Investment Bank**
FR   **BEI**   **Banque européenne d'investissement**
DE   **EIB**   **Europäische Investitionbank**
RU   **ЕИБ**   **Европейский инвестиционный банк**
ЕС

178
EN   **EIC**   **Euro Info Centre**

FR	EIC	Euro-Info-Centre; euroguichet
DE	EIC	EG-Beratungsstelle für Unternehmen
RU	-	Евро-Инфоцентр
		EC

179

EN	EIF	European Investment Fund
FR	FEI	Fonds européen d'investissement
DE	EIF	Europäischer Investitionsfonds
RU	ЕИФ	Европейский инвестиционный фонд
		EC

180

EN	EIN	European Informatics Network
FR	EIN	Réseau informatique européen
DE	EIN	Europäisches Informatiknetz
RU	-	Европейская информационная сеть

181

EN	EINECS	European Inventory of Existing Commercial Chemical Substances
FR	EINECS	Inventaire européen des substances commerciales existantes
DE	EINECS	Europäisches Verzeichnis der auf dem Markt vorhandenen chemischen Stoffe
RU	-	Европейский реестр химических веществ, находящихся в торговом обороте

182

EN	EIPA	European Institute of Public Administration
FR	IEAP	Institut européen d'administration publique
DE	-	Europäisches Institut für öffentliche Verwaltung
RU	-	Европейский институт государственного управления

183

EN	EIS	European Information System
FR	SIE	Système d'information européen
DE	EIS	Europäisches Informationssystem
RU	-	Европейская информационная система

184

EN	ELDR	Group of the European Liberal Democrat and Reform Party
FR	ELDR	groupe du Parti européen des libéraux démocrates et réformateurs
DE	ELDR	Fraktion der Liberalen und Demokratischen Partei Europas

RU	-	группа Европейской партии либеральных демократов и реформаторов *фракция в Европейском Парламенте*

185

EN	ELISE	European Information-exchange Network on Local Development and Local Employment Initiatives
FR	ELISE	Réseau européen d'echange d'informations sur le développement local et les initiatives locales d'emploi
DE	ELISE	Europäische Informationsaustauschnetz über lokale Entwicklung und lokale Arbeitsinitiativen
RU	-	Европейская система информации о проектах развития и занятости на местах *ЕС*

186

EN	ELISE	European Loan Insurance Scheme for Employment
FR	ELISE	Système européen d'assurance des emprunts pour l'emploi
DE	-	Europäisches System für Anleihe-Versicherung mit dem Ziel der Erhöhung der Beschäftigung
RU	-	Европейская система страхования займов в целях повышения занятости *форма финансового содействия ЕС мелким и средним предприятиям*

187

EN	EMA	European Monetary Agreement
FR	AME	Accord monétaire européen
DE	EWA	Europäisches Währungsabkommen
RU	ЕВС	Европейское валютное соглашение *система многосторонних расчетов между европейскими странами, созданная в 1955 г.*

188

EN	EMBO	European Molecular Biology Organization
FR	OEBM; EMBO	organisation européenne de biologie moléculaire
DE	EMBO	Europäische Molekularbiologie-Organisation
RU	ЕОМБ	Европейская организация молекулярной биологии

189

EN	EMCF	European Monetary Co-operation Fund
FR	FECOM	Fonds européen de coopération monétaire
DE	EFWZ	Europäischer Fonds für währungspolitische Zusammenarbeit
RU	ЕФВС	Европейский фонд валютного сотрудничества *ЕС*

190

EN	EMI	European Monetary Institute
FR	IME	Institut monétaire européen
DE	EWI	Europäisches Währungsinstitut
RU	ЕВИ	Европейский валютный институт
		EC

191

EN	EMS	European Monetary System
FR	SME	Système monétaire européen
DE	EWS	Europäisches Währungssystem
RU	ЕВС	Европейская валютная система
		EC

192

EN	EMU	Economic and Monetary Union
FR	UEM	Union économique et monétaire
DE	WWU	Wirtschafts- und Währungsunion
RU	ЭВС	Экономический и валютный союз

193

EN	EMUA	European Monetary Unit of Account
FR	UCME	unité de compte monétaire européenne
DE	EWRE	Europäische Währungsrechnungseinheit
RU	-	европейская валютная расчетная единица
		использовалась в рамках Европейского фонда валютного сотрудничества

194

EN	EN	European Norm (or Standard)
FR	EN	norme européenne
DE	-	europäischer Standard
RU	-	европейский стандарт

195

EN	ENEA	European Nuclear Energy Agency
FR	AEEN	Agence européenne pour l'énergie nucléaire
DE	ENEA	Europäische Kernenergie-Agentur
RU	-	Европейское агентство по ядерной энергии
		в настоящее время - Агентство по ядерной энергии (АЯЕ)

196

EN	ENVIREG	Community Initiative Contributing to Protection of the Environment and Promoting Economic Development
FR	ENVIREG	Initiative communautaire concernant la protection de l'environnement et favorisant le développement socio-économique

DE   **ENVIREG**   **Gemeinschaftsinitiative zur Verbesserung des Umweltschutzes und zur Förderung der Sozioökonomischen Entwicklung**

RU   -   Инициатива Сообщества в области охраны окружающей среды и содействия социально-экономическому развитию

197
EN   **EOQ**   **European Organization for Quality**
FR   **OEQ**   **Organisation européenne pour la qualité**
DE   **EOQ**   **Europäische Organisation für Qualität**
RU   -   **Европейская организация по качеству**

198
EN   **EOTA**   **European Organization for Technical Approvals**
FR   **EOTA**   **Organisation européenne pour l'agrément technique**
DE   **EOTA**   **Europäische Organisation für Technische Zulassungen**
RU   -   **Европейская организация по техническому соответствию**
                          выдает сертификаты соответствия европейским стандартам

199
EN   **EOTC**   **European Organization for Testing and Certification**
FR   **EOTC**   **Organisation européenne d'essais et de certification**
DE   **EOTC**   **Europäische Organisation für Zertifizierung und Prüfwesen**
RU   -   **Европейская организация по испытаниям и сертификации**

200
EN   **EP**   **European Parliament**
FR   **PE**   **Parlement européen**
DE   **EP**   **Europäisches Parlament**
RU   **ЕП**   **Европейский Парламент**
                          ЕС

201
EN   **EPC**   **Economic Policy Committee**
FR   **CPE**   **Comité de politique économique**
DE   **EPC**   **Wirtschaftpolitischer Ausschuss**
RU   -   Комитет по экономической политике
                          ЕС

202
EN   **EPC**   **European Patent Convention; Convention on the Grant of European Patents**
FR   **CBE**   **Convention sur le brevet européen; Convention sur la délivrance de brevets européens**

DE	**EPÜ**	Europäisches Patentübereinkommen; Übereinkommen über die Erteilung europäischer Patente
RU	-	Европейская патентная конвенция; Конвенция о выдаче европейских патентов

203

EN	**EPC**	European Political Co-operation
FR	**CPE**	coopération politique européenne
DE	**EPZ**	Europäische Politische Zusammenarbeit
RU	**ЕПС**	европейское политическое сотрудничество

204

EN	**EPI**	Institute of Professional Representatives before the European Patent Office
FR	**EPI**	Institut des mandataires agréés près l'Office européen des brevets
DE	**EPI**	Institut der beim Europäischen Patentamt zugelassenen Vertreter
RU	-	Институт уполномоченных при Европейском патентном бюро

205

EN	**EPO**	European Patent Office
FR	**OEB**	Office européen des brevets
DE	**EPA**	Europäisches Patentamt
RU	**ЕПВ**	Европейское патентное ведомство

206

EN	**EPO**	European Patent Organization
FR	**OEB**	Organisation européenne des brevets
DE	**EPO**	Europäische Patentorganisation
RU	**ЕПО**	Европейская патентная организация

207

EN	**EQO**	environmental quality objectives
FR	-	objectifs de qualité environnementaux
DE	**UQZ**	Umweltqualitätsziele
RU	-	ориентиры в отношении качества окружающей среды

208

EN	**EQS**	environmental quality standards
FR	**NQE**	normes de qualité environnementales
DE	**UQN**	Umweltqualitätsnormen
RU	-	стандарты качества окружающей среды

209

EN	**ERASMUS**	European Community Action Scheme for the Mobility of University Students

FR	ERASMUS	Programme d'action communautaire en matière de mobilité des étudiants
DE	ERASMUS	Aktionsprogramm der Europäischen Gemeinschaft zur Förderung der Mobilität von Hochschulstudenten
RU	ЭРАЗМУС	Программа действий Сообщества в целях поощрения мобильности студентов университетов

210
EN	ERC	European Radiocommunications Committee
FR	ERC	Comité européen des radiocommunications
DE	ERC	Europäisches Funkverbindungs-Komitee
RU	-	Европейский комитет радиосвязи

211
EN	ERC	European Reference Centre
FR	CRE	centre de référence européen
DE	ERZ	Europäisches Referenzzentrum
RU	-	европейский информационный центр *ЕС*

212
EN	ERDF	European Regional Development Fund
FR	FEDER	Fonds européen de développement régional
DE	EFRE	Europäischer Fonds für regionale Entwicklung
RU	ЕФРР	Европейский фонд регионального развития *ЕС*

213
EN	ERGO	European Community Action Programme for the Long-term Unemployed
FR	ERGO	Programme d'action communautaire en faveur des chômeurs de longue durée
DE	ERGO	Aktionsprogramm der Europäischen Gemeinschaft zur Bekämpfung der Langzeitarbeitslosigkeit
RU	-	Программа действий Европейского сообщества в поддержку лиц, не имеющих работы в течение длительного времени

214
EN	ERM	exchange-rate mechanism
FR	-	mécanisme de change
DE	-	Umrechnungskursmechanismus
RU	-	курсовой механизм *(Европейской валютной системы)*

215
| EN | ESA | European Space Agency |
| FR | ASE | Agence spatiale européenne |

| DE | EWO | Europäische Weltraumorganisation |
| RU | EKA | Европейское космическое агентство |

216
EN	ESA	Euratom Supply Agency
FR	AA	Agence d'approvisionnement d'Euratom
DE	-	Euratom-Versorgungsagentur
RU	-	Агентство по снабжению Евратома
		(расщепляющимися материалами)

217
EN	ESA	European System of Integrated Economic Accounts
FR	SEC	Système européen de comptes économiques intégrés
DE	ESVG	Europäisches System Volkswirtschaftlicher Gesamtrechnungen
RU	-	Европейская система интегрированных экономических счетов
		EC

218
EN	ESC	Economic and Social Committee
FR	CES	Comité économique et social
DE	WSA	Wirtschafts- und Sozialausschuss
RU	ЕСК	Экономический и социальный комитет
		EC

219
EN	ESCB	European System of Central Banks
FR	SEBC	Système européen de banques centrales
DE	EZBS	Europäisches Zentralbanksystem
RU	ЕСЦБ	Европейская система центральных банков
		предусмотрена Договором о Европейском Союзе

220
EN	ESF	European Science Foundation
FR	FES	Fondation européenne de la science
DE	EWS	Europäische Wissenschaftsstiftung
RU	-	Европейский научный фонд
		EC

221
EN	ESF	European Social Fund
FR	FSE	Fonds social européen
DE	ESF	Europäischer Sozialfonds
RU	-	Европейский социальный фонд
		EC

222
| EN | ESPRI | European Economic and Social Policy Research Institute |

FR **IRPES** Institut européen de recherche sur les politiques
économiques et sociales
DE **EFWS** Das Europäische Forschungsinstitut für Wirtschafts-
und Sozialpolitik
RU - Европейский научно-исследовательский институт
экономической и социальной политики

223
EN **ESPRIT** European Strategic Programme for Research and
Development in Information Technologies
FR **ESPRIT** Programme européen stratégique de recherche et de
développement dans le domaine des technologies de
l'information
DE **ESPRIT** Europäisches strategisches Forschungs- und
Entwicklungsprogramm auf dem Gebiet der
Informationstechnologien
RU **ЭСПРИТ** Европейская стратегическая программа
исследований и разработок в сфере
информационных технологий
EC

224
EN **ESRIN** European Space Research Institute
FR **ESRIN** Institut européen de recherches spatiales
DE **ESRIN** Europäisches Institut für Weltraumforschung
RU - Европейский институт космических исследований

225
EN **ETA** European technical approval
FR **ATE** agrément technique européen
DE - europäische technische Zustimmung
RU - признание соответствия европейским стандартам

226
EN **ETC** European Transport Committee
FR **CET** Comité européen des transports
DE **CET** Europäischer Verkehrsausschuss
RU - Европейский комитет по транспорту

227
EN **ETS** European telecommunication standard
FR **NET** norme européenne de télécommunication
DE **ETS** Europäische Telekommunikationsnorm
RU - европейский стандарт в области
телекоммуникаций

228
EN **ETSC** European Transport Safety Council
FR **CEST** Conseil européen pour la sécurité en transport

| DE | - | Europäischer Rat zur Sicherung der Transportwesen |
| RU | - | Европейский совет по безопасности на транспорте |

229
EN	ETSI	European Telecommunications Standards Institute
FR	ETSI; IENT	Institut européen de normalisation des télécommunications
DE	ETSI	Europäisches Institut für Telekommunikationsnormen
RU	-	Европейский институт стандартизации в области телекоммуникаций

230
EN	ETUC	European Trade Union Confederation
FR	CES	Confédération européenne des syndicats
DE	EGB	Europäischer Gewerkschaftsbund
RU	-	Европейская конфедерация профессиональных союзов
		ЕС

231
EN	EU	European Union
FR	UE	Union européenne
DE	EU	Europäische Union
RU	ЕС	Европейский Союз

232
EN	EUA	European Unit of Account
FR	UCE	unité de compte européenne
DE	ERE	Europäische Rechnungseinheit
RU	ЕРЕ	европейская расчетная единица

233
EN	EUI	European University Institute
FR	IUE	Institut universitaire européen
DE	EHI	Europäisches Hochschulinstitut
RU	-	Европейский университетский институт
		ЕС

234
EN	EURAM	European Research on Advanced Materials
FR	EURAM	Recherche européenne sur les matériaux avancés
DE	EURAM	Forschungsprogramm über Materialen
RU	ЕВРАМ	Европейские исследования новых видов материалов
		программа исследований ЕС в области технологии материалов

235
| EN | EUREKA | European Research Co-ordination Agency |

FR	EUREKA	Agence européenne pour la coordination de la recherche
DE	EUREKA	Europäische Agentur über Koordinierung der Wissenschaftsforschung
RU	ЭВРИКА	Европейское агентство по координации научных исследований

236
EN	EURES	European Employment Services
FR	EURES	Service européen d'emploi
DE	EURES	Europäisches Netz für Stellenangebote
RU	-	Европейская служба занятости

распространяет информацию о вакансиях в странах ЕС

237
EN	EURESCOM	European Research and Strategic Planning Institute
FR	EURESCOM	Institut européen de recherche et de planification stratégique
DE	EURESCOM	Europäisches Institut für Forschung und Strategische Planung
RU	-	Европейский институт научных исследований и стратегического планирования

238
EN	EURET	European Research for Transport; Specific Research and Technological Development Programme in the field of Transport
FR	EURET	Programme spécifique de recherche et de développement technologique dans le domaine des transports
DE	EURET	Spezifisches Programm für Forschung und technologische Entwicklung im Verkehrswesen
RU	ЕВРЕТ	Европейские исследования для транспорта; Специальная научно-техническая программа ЕС в области транспорта

239
EN	EURISTOTE	Computerized Information System on University Research relating to European Integration
FR	EURISTOTE	Système d'information informatisé sur les recherches universitaires sur l'intégration européenne
DE	EURISTOTE	Rechnergestütztes Informationssystem über Hochschuluntersuchungen und Forschungen über die europäische Integration
RU	ЭРИСТОТ	Компьютеризированная система информации об университетских научных исследованиях по европейской интеграции

программа ЕС

240
EN EUROCHAMBRES Association of European Chambers of Commerce and
Industry
FR EUROCHAMBRES Association des chambres de commerce et d'industrie
européennes
DE - Dachorganisation der Industrie-u. Handelskammern
der EG und der EFTA
RU - Ассоциация европейских торгово-промышленных
палат
профессиональная организация в ЕС

241
EN EUROCONTROL European Organization for the Safety of Air
Navigation
FR EUROCONTROL Organisation européenne pour la sécurité de la
navigation aérienne
DE EUROCONTROL Europäische Organisation zur Sicherung der Luftfahrt
RU ЕВРОКОНТРОЛ Европейская организация по безопасности
воздушной навигации

242
EN EURO COOP European Community of Consumer Co-operatives
FR EURO COOP Communauté européenne des coopératives de
consommation
DE EURO COOP Europäische Gemeinschaft der
Konsumgenossenschaften
RU - Европейское сообщество потребительских
кооперативов

243
EN EUROCOPI European Computer Programme Institute
FR EUROCOPI Institut européen pour les programmes d'ordinateurs
DE EUROCOPI Europäisches Institut für Computerprogramme
RU - Европейский институт компьютерных программ

244
EN EUROCOTON Committee of the Cotton and Allied Textile Industries
of the EEC
FR EUROCOTON Comité des industries du coton et des fibres connexes de
la CEE
DE EUROCOTON Komitee der Baumwoll- und verwandten
Textilindustrien der EWG
RU ЕВРОКОТОН Комитет по хлопчатобумажной и смежным
отраслям текстильной промышленности ЕЭС

245
EN EUROFER European Confederation of the Iron and Steel Industry

FR	EUROFER	Association européenne de la sidérurgie
DE	EUROFER	Europäische Wirtschaftsvereinigung Eisen- und Stahlindustrie
RU	ЕВРОФЕР	Европейская конфедерация черной металлургии *профессиональная организация в ЕС*

246
EN	EUROFORM	Community Initiative concerning New Qualifications, New Skills and New Employment Opportunities
FR	EUROFORM	Initiative communautaire concernant les nouvelles qualifications, les nouvelles compétences et les nouvelles opportunités d'emploi
DE	EUROFORM	Gemeinschaftsinitiative über neue Berufsqualifikationen, Fachkenntnisse und Beschäftigungsmöglichkeiten
RU	ЕВРОФОРМ	Инициатива Сообщества в целях содействия профессиональной подготовке и занятости *программа ЕС*

247
EN	EuronAid	European Association of Non-governmental Organizations for Food and Emergency Aid
FR	EuronAid	Association européenne d'organisations non gouvernementales d'aide alimentaire et d'urgence
DE	EuronAid	Europäische Vereinigung der Nichtregierungsorganisationen für Nahrungsmittel- und Nothilfe
RU	-	Европейская ассоциация неправительственных организаций по оказанию продовольственной и чрезвычайной помощи

248
EN	EUROPECHE	Association of National Organizations of Fishing Enterprises of EC
FR	EUROPECHE	Association des organisations nationales d'entreprises de pêche de la CE
DE	EUROPECHE	Vereinigung der nationalen Verbände von Fischereiunternehmern in der EG
RU	-	Ассоциация национальных организаций рыболовных предприятий ЕС

249
EN	Europol	European Police Office
FR	Europol	Office européen de police
DE	Europol	Europäisches Polizeiamt
RU	Европол	Европейское полицейское управление *ЕС*

250
EN	**EUROS**	**European Community Ship Register**
FR	-	**Registre des navires de la Communauté européenne**
DE	-	**Europäisches Schiffsregister**
RU	-	**Судовой регистр Европейского сообщества**

251
EN	**EUROSTAT; SOEC**	**Statistical Office of the European Communities**
FR	**EUROSTAT; OSCE**	**Office statistique des Communautés européennes**
DE	**EUROSTAT; SAEG**	**Statistisches Amt der Europäischen Gemeinschaften**
RU	**ЕВРОСТАТ**	**Статистическое бюро Европейских сообществ**

252
EN	**EUROTECNET**	European Technologies Network; Action Programme to Promote Innovation in the field of Vocational Training resulting from Technological Changes in the European Community
FR	**EUROTECNET**	Programme d'action visant à promouvoir l'innovation dans le domaine de la formation professionnelle résultant du changement technologique dans la Communauté européenne
DE	**EUROTECNET**	Aktionsprogramm zur Förderung von Innovationen in der Berufsbildung in der Folge des technologischen Wandels in der Europäischen Gemeinschaft
RU	**ЕВРОТЕКНЕТ**	Европейская технологическая система; Программа содействия нововведениям в профессиональной подготовке в связи с развитием технологии в Европейском сообществе

253
EN	**EUROTRA**	European Economic Community Research and Development Programme for a Machine Translation System of Advanced Design
FR	**EUROTRA**	Programme de recherche et de développement pour la Communauté économique européenne, relatif à un système de traduction automatique de conception avancée
DE	**EUROTRA**	Forschungs- und Entwicklungsprogramm der Europäischen Wirtschaftsgemeinschaft für ein automatisches Übersetzungssystem modernster Konzeption
RU	**ЕВРОТРА**	Программа ЕЭС по созданию системы автоматизированного перевода на базе передовой технологии

254
EN **EURYDICE** Education Information Network in the European Community
FR **EURYDICE** Réseau d'information sur l'éducation dans la Communauté européenne
DE **EURYDICE** Bildungsinformationsnetz in der Europäischen Gemeinschaft
RU **-** Система информации в ЕС по вопросам образования
программа ЕС

255
EN **EUTELSAT** European Telecommunications Satellite Organization
FR **EUTELSAT** Organisation européenne de télécommunications par satellite
DE **EUTELSAT** Europäische Fernmeldesatellitenorganisation
RU **ЭТЕЛСАТ** Европейская организация по спутниковой связи

256
EN **EUVP** European Union Visitors Programme
FR **EUVP** Programme de visites de l'Union européenne
DE **EUVP** Das Besucherprogramm der Europäischen Union
RU **-** Программа визитов Европейского Союза

257
EN **EVCA** European Venture Capital Association
FR **EVCA/AECR** Association européenne de capital à risque
DE **EVCA** Europäische Vereinigung des Risikokapitals
RU **-** Европейская ассоциация "рискового" капитала
профессиональное объединение банков и фирм, специализирующихся на "рисковом" финансировании

258
EN **EYC** European Youth Centre
FR **CEJ** Centre européen de la jeunesse
DE **CEJ** Europäisches Jugendzentrum
RU **-** Европейский центр молодежи

259
EN **EYF** European Youth Foundation
FR **FEJ** Fonds européen pour la jeunesse
DE **EJW** Europäisches Jugendwerk
RU **-** Европейский молодежный фонд

260
EN **FADN** Farm Accountancy Data Network
FR **RICA** Réseau d'information comptable agricole
DE **INLB** Informationsnetz landwirtschaftlicher Buchführungen

RU - система бухгалтерских данных по сельскому
хозяйству
применяется Европейской Комиссией

261
EN **FAO** Food and Agriculture Organization of the United
Nations
FR **OAA; FAO** Organisation des Nations unies pour l'alimentation et
l'agriculture
DE **FAO** Ernährungs- und Landwirtschafts-Organisation der
Vereinten Nationen
RU **ФАО** Продовольственная и сельскохозяйственная
организация Объединенных Наций

262
EN **FAST** Forecasting and Assessment in the field of Science and
Technology
FR **FAST** Prévision et évalution dans le domaine de la science et
de la technologie
DE **FAST** Vorausschau und Bewertung in Wissenschaft und
Technologie
RU **ФАСТ** Прогнозирование и оценка результатов
деятельности в сфере науки и техники
программа ЕС

263
EN **FDI** foreign direct investments
FR **IDE** investissements directs étrangers
DE - ausländische direktinvestitionen
RU **ПИИ** прямые иностранные инвестиции

264
EN **FIFG** Financial Instrument for Fisheries Guidance
FR **IFOP** instrument financier d'orientation de la pêche
DE **FIAF** Finanzinstrument für die Ausrichtung der Fischerei
RU - финансовый инструмент структурной политики в
области рыболовства
ЕС

265
EN **FLAIR** Food-linked Agro-industrial Research; Specific
Research and Technological Development Programme
in the Field of Food Science and Technology
FR **FLAIR** Programme spécifique de recherche et de
développement dans le domaine des sciences et des
technologies de l'alimentation
DE **FLAIR** Spezifisches Programm für Forschung und
technologische Entwicklung auf dem Gebiet der
Lebensmittelwissenschaft und -technologie

RU ФЛЭР Исследования в агропромышленном секторе, касающиеся продовольствия; Специальная научно-техническая программа в области пищевой промышленности
ЕС

266
EN FOD French Overseas Departments
FR DFOM départements français d'outre-mer
DE - Frankreichsüberseeische Departments
RU - заморские департаменты Франции

267
EN FORCE Action Programme for the Development of Continuing Vocational Training in the European Community
FR FORCE Programme d'action pour le développement de la formation professionnelle continue dans la Communauté européenne
DE FORCE Aktionsprogramm der Gemeinschaft zur Förderung der beruflichen Weiterbildung
RU ФОРС Программа содействия повышению профессиональной подготовки в Европейском сообществе

268
EN FSU former Soviet Union
FR - ex-URSS
DE - ehem. Sowetunion
RU - бывший Советский Союз

269
EN FTA free-trade area
FR ZLE zone de libre-échange
DE FHZ Freihandelszone
RU ЗСТ зона свободной торговли

270
EN FTC financial and technical co-operation
FR CFT coopération financière et technique
DE - Finanzielle und technische Zusammenarbeit
RU - финансовое и техническое сотрудничество

271
EN G-7 Group of Seven
FR G-7; G7 Groupe des Sept
DE G7- gruppen Gruppe der Sieben
RU - Группа семи
"большая семерка"

272
EN	G 77	Group of 77
FR	G 77	Groupe des 77
DE	G 77	Gruppe der 77
RU	-	Группа 77

развивающиеся страны, ЮНКТАД

273
EN	GATS	General Agreement on Trade in Services
FR	GATS	Accord général sur le commerce des services
DE	GATS	Allgemeines Abkommen über den Handel mit Dienstleistungen
RU	ГАТС	Генеральное соглашение по торговле услугами

ВТО

274
EN	GATT	General Agreement on Tariffs and Trade
FR	GATT	Accord général sur les tarifs douaniers et le commerce
DE	GATT	Allgemeines Zoll- und Handelsabkommen
RU	ГАТТ	Генеральное соглашение по тарифам и торговле

ВТО

275
EN	GDP	gross domestic product
FR	PIB	produit intérieur brut
DE	BIP	Bruttoinlandsprodukt
RU	ВВП	валовой внутренний продукт

276
EN	GDPmp	gross domestic product at market prices
FR	PIBpm	produit intérieur brut aux prix du marché
DE	-	Bruttoinlandprodukt zu Marktpreisen
RU	-	валовой внутренний продукт в рыночных ценах

277
EN	GDS	geographically disadvantaged States
FR	GDS	Etats géographiquement désavantagés
DE	GDS	durch ihre geographische Lage benachteiligte Staaten
RU	-	страны с неблагоприятным географическим положением

278
EN	GGF	Global Governmental Forum
FR	GGF	Forum gouvernemental global
DE	-	Globales Zwischenstaatliches Forum
RU	-	Глобальный межправительственный форум

организация, создаваемая по инициативе ЕС, США и Японии в целях либерализации торговли полупроводниками

279

EN	GL	guide level
FR	NG	niveau guide
DE	RZ	Richtzahl
RU	-	ориентировочный уровень
		(цен, объема производства/импорта)

280

EN	GNP	gross national product
FR	PNB	produit national brut
DE	BSP	Bruttosozialprodukt
RU	ВНП	валовой национальный продукт

281

EN	GNPmp	gross national product at market prices
FR	PNBpm	produit national brut aux prix du marché
DE	BSPmp	Bruttosozialprodukt zu Marktpreisen
RU	-	валовой национальный продукт в рыночных ценах

282

EN	GPT	generalized preferential tariff
FR	TPG	tarif de préférence générale
DE	-	Tarif des Allgemeinen Systems der Preferenzen
RU	-	таможенные пошлины, применяемые в рамках Общей системы преференций
		(развитых стран в пользу развивающихся)

283

EN	GRUCA	Central American Ambassadors' Group to the EC
FR	GRUCA	groupe des ambassadeurs centraméricains auprès de la CE
DE	-	Gruppe der zentralamerikanischen Botschafter bei der EU
RU	-	Группа послов центральноамериканских стран при ЕС

284

EN	GRULA	Latin American Group; Group of Latin American Ambassadors
FR	GRULA	Groupe latino-américain; groupe des ambassadeurs latino-américains
DE	GRULA	Gruppe der lateinamerikanischen Botschafter
RU	ГРУЛА	Латиноамериканская группа; Группа послов латиноамериканских стран
		(при ЕС)

285

EN	GSTP	Global System of Trade Preferences
FR	SGPC; GSTP	système global de préférences commerciales

DE	-	Globales System der Handelspreferenzen
RU	ГСТП	глобальная система торговых преференций
		(между развивающимися странами)

286
EN	GUE/NGL	Confederal Group of the European United Left/Nordic Green Left
FR	GUE/NGL	groupe confédéral de la Gauche unitaire européenne/ Gauche verte nordique
DE	GUE/NGL	Konföderale Fraktion der Vereinigten Europäischen Linken/Nordische Grüne Linke
RU	-	Конфедеральная группа европейских объединенных левых и ''зеленых'' левых северных стран
		фракция в Европейском Парламенте

287
EN	GVW; MATW; MAW	permitted gross vehicle weight; maximum authorized total weight; maximum authorized weight
FR	PMA; PTC; PTMA; PTAC	poids maximals autorisé en charge; poids total en charge; poids total maximum autorisé; poids total autorisé en charge
DE	-	höchstzulässiges Gesamtgewicht
RU	-	максимально допустимый общий вес грузовика
		ЕС

288
EN	HA	High Authority
FR	HA	Haute Autorité
DE	-	Oberstes Organ
RU	-	Верховный орган
		ЕОУС, до 1967 г.

289
EN	HDTV	high-definition TV
FR	TVHD	télévision à haute définition
DE	HDTV	hochauflösendes Fernsehen
RU	-	телевидение высокой четкости изображения

290
EN	HELIOS	Handicapped People in the European Community Living Independently in an Open Society; Community Action Programme to Assist Disabled People
FR	HELIOS	Programme d'action communautaire en faveur des personnes handicapées
DE	HELIOS	Drittes Aktionsprogramm der Gemeinschaft zugunsten der Behinderten

RU	-	Физически неполноценные лица в Европейском сообществе, живущие независимо в открытом обществе; Программа Сообщества по оказанию помощи инвалидам

291

EN	HS	Harmonized Commodity Description and Coding System
FR	SH	Système harmonisé de désignation et de codification des marchandises
DE	HS	Harmonisiertes System für Waren Beschreibung und Kodierung
RU	ГС	Гармонизированная система описания и кодирования товаров

292

EN	HST	high-speed train
FR	TGV	train à grande vitesse
DE	-	Hochschnellzug
RU	-	высокоскоростной поезд

293

EN	IAEA	International Atomic Energy Agency
FR	AIEA	Agence internationale de l'énergie atomique
DE	IAEO	Internationale Atomenergie-Organisation
RU	МАГАТЭ	Международное агентство по атомной энергии *ООН*

294

EN	IBRD	International Bank for Reconstruction and Development (World Bank)
FR	BIRD	Banque internationale pour la reconstruction et le développement (Banque mondiale)
DE	IBRD	Internationale Bank für Wiederaufbau und Entwicklung (Weltbank)
RU	МБРР	Международный банк реконструкции и развития (Мировой банк) *ООН*

295

EN	ICA	international commodity agreement or arrangement
FR	AIP	accord ou arrangement international de produit
DE	-	Internationales Rohstoffübereinkommen; Internationale Rohstoffvereinbarung
RU	-	международное товарное соглашение

296

EN	ICA	International Co-operative Alliance
FR	ACI	Alliance coopérative internationale

DE	**IGB**	**Internationaler Genossenschaftsbund**
RU	**МКА**	**Международный кооперативный альянс**

297
EN	**ICC**	**International Chamber of Commerce**
FR	**CCI**	**Chambre de commerce internationale**
DE	**IHK**	**Internationale Handelskammer**
RU	**МТП**	**Международная торговая палата**

298
EN	**ICCP**	**Information, Computers and Communications Policy**
FR	**PIIC**	**politique de l'information, de l'informatique et des communications**
DE	**ICCP**	**Informations-, Datenverarbeitungs- und Fernmeldepolitik**
RU	**-**	**Политика в области информации, информатики и связи** *ЕС*

299
EN	**ICIA**	**International Credit Insurance Association**
FR	**ICIA**	**Association internationale des assureurs-crédit**
DE	**ICIA**	**Internationale Kreditversicherungs-Vereinigung**
RU	**-**	**Международная ассоциация по страхованию кредитов**

300
EN	**ICJ**	**International Court of Justice**
FR	**CIJ**	**Cour internationale de justice**
DE	**IGH**	**Internationaler Gerichtshof**
RU	**-**	**Международный суд** *(в Гааге)*

301
EN	**ICONE**	**Comparative Index of National and European Standards**
FR	**ICONE**	**Index comparatif des normes nationales et européennes**
DE	**-**	**Vergleichender Index der nationalen und europäischen Standards**
RU	**-**	**Сравнительный перечень национальных и европейских стандартов**

302
EN	**ICSID**	**International Centre for Settlement of Investment Disputes**
FR	**CIRDI**	**Centre international pour le règlement des différends relatifs aux investissements**
DE	**ICSID**	**Internationales Zentrum zur Beilegung von Investitionsstreitigkeiten**

RU	МЦУИС	Международный центр по урегулированию инвестиционных споров

303

EN	IDA	Interchange of Data between Administrations
FR	IDA	échange de données entre administrations
DE	IDA	Datenaustausch zwischen Verwaltungen
RU	-	обмен данными между администрациями *(стран ЕС)*

304

EN	IDA	International Development Association
FR	AID	Association internationale pour le développement
DE	IDA	Internationale Entwicklungsorganisation
RU	MAP	Международная ассоциация развития

305

EN	IDO	integrated development operation
FR	OID	opération intégrée de développement
DE	-	Integrierte Transaktion für Entwicklung
RU	-	интегрированная операция в целях развития

306

EN	IEA	International Energy Agency
FR	AIE	Agence internationale de l'énergie
DE	IEA	Internationale Energie-Agentur
RU	МЭА	Международное энергетическое агентство *ОЭСР*

307

EN	IFA	International Fiscal Association
FR	IFA	Association fiscale internationale
DE	IFA	Internationale Vereinigung für Steuerrecht
RU	-	Международная налоговая ассоциация

308

EN	IGC	inter-governmental conference
FR	CIG	conférence intergouvernementale
DE	-	Zwischenstaatliche Konferenz
RU	-	межправительственная конференция *(стран-членов ЕС)*

309

EN	IGC-PU	Intergovernmental Conference - Political Union
FR	CIG-UP	Conférence intergouvernementale - Union politique
DE	-	Zwischenstaatliche Konferenz - Politische Union
RU	-	Межправительственная конференция - вопросы политического союза

310
EN	**IGO**	**intergovernmental organization**
FR	**OIG**	**organisation intergouvernementale**
DE	**-**	**zwischenstaatliche Organisation**
RU	**-**	**межправительственная организация**

311
EN	**IIIA**	**International Investment Insurance Agency**
FR	**AIAI**	**Agence internationale d'assurance des investissements**
DE	**IAIV**	**Internationale Agentur für Investitionsversicherung**
RU	**-**	**Международное агентство по страхованию инвестиций**

312
EN	**ILO**	**International Labour Organization**
FR	**OIT**	**Organisation internationale du travail**
DE	**IAO**	**Internationale Arbeitsorganisation**
RU	**МОТ**	**Международная организация труда** *ООН*

313
EN	**IMF**	**International Monetary Fund**
FR	**FMI**	**Fonds monétaire international**
DE	**IWF**	**Internationaler Währungsfonds**
RU	**МВФ**	**Международный валютный фонд** *ООН*

314
EN	**IMPACT**	**Information Market Policy Actions; plan of action for setting up an information services market**
FR	**IMPACT**	**Plan d'action pour la création d'un marché des services de l'information**
DE	**IMPACT**	**Aktionsplan zur Schaffung eines Marktes für Informationsdienste**
RU	**-**	**План действий по созданию рынка информационных услуг** *ЕС*

315
EN	**IMPs**	**Integrated Mediterranean Programmes**
FR	**PIM**	**programmes intégrés méditerranéens**
DE	**IMP**	**Integrierte Mittelmeerprogramme**
RU	**-**	**интегрированные средиземноморские программы** *программы комплексного финансирования наименее развитых средиземноморских регионов Сообщества*

316
EN	**INGO**	**international non-governmental organization**

FR	**OING**	organisation internationale non gouvernementale
DE	-	internationale nichtstaatliche Organisation
RU	-	международная неправительственная организация

317

EN	**INTERLAINE**	Committee for the Wool Textile Industry in the EEC
FR	**INTERLAINE**	Comité des industries lainières de la CEE
DE	**INTERLAINE**	Ausschuss der Wollindustrien der EWG
RU	-	Комитет шерстяной промышленности ЕЭС
		профессиональная организация

318

EN	**Interreg**	Community Initiative concerning Border Areas
FR	**Interreg**	Initiative communautaire concernant les zones frontalières
DE	-	Gemeinschaftsinitiative über die Grenzzonen
RU	-	Инициатива Сообщества, касающаяся пограничных зон

319

EN	**I/O**	input/output
FR	**E/S**	entrée/sortie
DE	-	Produktionsaufwand/Produktionsausstoss
RU	-	затраты производства/выпуск продукции

320

EN	**IP**	intellectual property
FR	**PI**	propriété intellectuelle
DE	-	Geistiges Eigentum
RU	**ИС**	интеллектуальная собственность

321

EN	**IPA**	inward processing arrangements
FR	**RPA**	régime de perfectionnement actif
DE	**AVV**	aktiver Veredelungsverkehr
RU	-	режим ввоза товаров для переработки *(с последующим вывозом)*

322

EN	**IPC**	Integrated Programme for Commodities
FR	**PIPB**	Programme intégré pour les produits de base
DE	**IGP**	Integriertes Grundstoffprogramm
RU	-	Интегрированная программа по сырьевым товарам *ЮНКТАД*

323

EN	**IPT**	inward processing traffic
FR	**TPA**	trafic de perfectionnement actif

| DE | AVV | aktiver Veredelungsverkehr |
| RU | - | ввоз товара с целью его переработки |

324

EN	IRDAC; CORDI	Industrial Research and Development Advisory Committee; Advisory Committee on Industrial Research and Development
FR	CORDI; IRDAC	Comité consultatif de la recherche et du développement industriels
DE	IRDAC	Beratender Ausschuss für Industrielle Forschung und Entwicklung
RU	ИРДАК	Консультативный комитет по промышленным исследованиям и разработкам *ЕС*

325

EN	IREPC	Implementing Regulations to the European Patent Convention
FR	RECBE	règlement d'exécution relatif à la Convention sur le brevet européen
DE	AO EPÜ	Ausführungsordnung zum europäischen Patentübereinkommen
RU	-	Правила применения Европейской патентной конвенции

326

EN	IRIS	Integrated Road Safety, Information and Navigation System
FR	IRIS	Système intégré de sécurité routière, d'information et de navigation
DE	-	Integriertes System der Strassensicherheit, Information und Verkehrsverwaltung
RU	АЙРИС	Интегрированная система дорожной безопасности, информации и управления движением *программа ЕС*

327

EN	ISIC	International Standard Industrial Classification of all Economic Activities
FR	CITI	Classification internationale type, par industrie, de toutes les branches d'activité économique
DE	ISIC	Internationale Systematik der wirtschaftlichen Tätigkeiten
RU	-	Международная стандартная классификация экономической деятельности по отраслям

328

| EN | ISO | International Organization for Standardization |

FR	**ISO**	**Organisation internationale de normalisation**
DE	**ISO**	**Internationale Normenorganisation**
RU	**ИСО**	**Международная организация по стандартизации**

329

EN	**ITC**	**International Trade Centre**
FR	**CCI**	**Centre du commerce international**
DE	**ITC**	**Internationales Handelszentrum**
RU	**МТЦ**	**Международный торговый центр**
		ВТО/ЮНКТАД

330

EN	**ITER**	international thermonuclear experimental reactor
FR	**ITER**	réacteur thermonucléaire expérimental international
DE	**ITER**	Internationaler thermonuklearer Versuchsreaktor
RU	**-**	международный экспериментальный термоядерный реактор
		совместный проект Евратома, России, США и Японии

331

EN	**JAF**	COST Working Party on Legal, Administrative and Financial Questions
FR	**JAF**	groupe COST des questions juridiques, administratives et financières
DE	**JAF**	COST-Arbeitsgruppe für Rechts-, Verwaltungs- und Finanzfragen
RU	**-**	рабочая группа КОСТ по юридическим, административным и финансовым вопросам

332

EN	**JANUS**	Community Information System for Health and Safety at Work
FR	**JANUS**	Système d'information communautaire pour la santé et la sécurité au travail
DE	**-**	Informationssystem der Gemeinschaft für Gesundheit und Sicherheit am Arbeitsplatz
RU	**-**	Информационная система Сообщества по вопросам здравоохранения и безопасности труда
		программа ЕС

333

EN	**JC**	judicial co-operation
FR	**CJ**	coopération judiciaire
DE	**-**	Zusammenarbeit in Rechtspflege
RU	**-**	сотрудничество в сфере правосудия

334

EN	**JEP**	Joint European Project

FR	-	projet européen commun
DE	-	Gemeinsameuropäisches Projekt
RU	-	совместный европейский проект

335

EN	JET	Joint European Torus
FR	JET	Joint European Torus
DE	JET	Forschungsprojekt der Gemeinschaft auf dem Gebiet der Kernfusion
RU	ДЖЕТ	Совместный европейский проект "Торус" *термоядерный реактор ЕС*

336

EN	JHA	Justice and home affaires
FR	JAI	justice et affaires intérieurs
DE	-	Rechtspflege und Innenangelegenheiten
RU	-	правосудие и внутренние дела

337

EN	JICS	Joint Interpreting and Conference Service
FR	SCIC	Service commun interprétation-conférences
DE	SCIC	Gemeinsamer Dolmetscher-Konferenzdienst
RU	-	Совместная служба переводов и проведения конференций *ЕС*

338

EN	JNRC	Joint Nuclear Research Centre
FR	CCRN	Centre commun de recherches nucléaires
DE	GKFS	Gemeinsame Kernforschungstelle
RU	-	Объединенный центр ядерных исследований *ЕС, до 1979 г.*

339

EN	JOULE	Joint Opportunities for Unconventional or Long-term Energy Supply; Specific Research and Technological Development Programme in the field of Non-nuclear Energy
FR	JOULE	Programme spécifique de recherche et de développement technologique dans le domaine des énergies non nucléaires
DE	JOULE	Spezifisches Programm für Forschung und technologische Entwicklung im Bereich der nichtnuklearen Energien
RU	ДЖОУЛЬ	Общие возможности для безусловного и долгосрочного снабжения энергией; Специальная научно-техническая программа в области неядерных источников энергии *ЕС*

340

EN	JRC	Joint Research Centre
FR	CCR	Centre commun de recherche
DE	GFS	Gemeinsame Forschungsstelle
RU	-	Объединенный исследовательский центр

ЕС, с 1979 г.

341

EN	KAROLUS	Action plan for the exchange between Member State administrations of national officials who are engaged in the implementation of Community legislation required to achieve the internal market
FR	KAROLUS	Plan d'action pour l'échange, entre les administrations des Etats membres, de fonctionnaires nationaux chargés de la mise en oeuvre de la législation communautaire nécessaire à la réalisation du marché intérieur
DE	KAROLUS	Aktionsplan für den zwischen den Verwaltungen der Mitgliedstaaten vozunehmenden Austausch nationaler Beamten, die mit der zur Verwirklichung des Binnenmarktes erforderlichen Durchführung des Gemeinschaftsrechts betraut sind
RU	-	План действий по обмену между администрациями государств-членов национальными должностными лицами, на которых возложено применение законодательства Сообщества, необходимого для завершения формирования внутреннего рынка

342

EN	LAA	Latin America and Asia
FR	ALA	Amérique Latine et Asie
DE	-	Lateinamerika und Asien
RU	ЛАА	Латинская Америка и Азия

343

EN	LAES; SELA	Latin American Economic System
FR	SELA	Système économique latino-américain
DE	-	Lateinamerikanisches Wirtschaftssystem
RU	ЛАЭС	Латиноамериканская экономическая система

344

EN	LAFTA	Latin American Free Trade Association
FR	-	Association latino-américaine de libre échange
DE	ALALC; LAFTA	Lateinamerikanische Freihandelszone
RU	ЛАСТ	Латиноамериканская ассоциация свободной торговли

(с 1980 г. Латиноамериканская ассоциация интеграции)

345

EN	**LAIA**	**Latin-American Integration Association**
FR	**ALADI**	**Association latino-américaine d'intégration**
DE	**-**	**Lateinamerikanische Integrationsassoziation**
RU	**ЛАИ**	**Латиноамериканская ассоциация интеграции**
		(до 1980 г. Латиноамериканская ассоциация свободной торговли)

346

EN	**LAS**	**League of Arab States**
FR	**LEA**	**Ligue des Etats arabes**
DE	**-**	**Arabische Liga**
RU	**ЛАГ**	**Лига арабских государств**

347

EN	**LDC**	**least developed countries**
FR	**PMD; PMA**	**pays les moins développés; pays les moins avancés**
DE	**LDC**	**am wenigsten entwickelte Länder; am wenigsten fortgeschrittene Länder**
RU	**-**	**наименее развитые страны**

348

EN	**LIC**	**low-income country**
FR	**PFR; PRF**	**pays à faible revenu; pays à revenu faible**
DE	**LIC**	**Länder mit niedrigem Einkommen; Niedrigeinkommen-Land**
RU	**-**	**страна с низким доходом**

349

EN	**LIFE**	**Financial Instrument for the Environment**
FR	**LIFE**	**Instrument financier pour l'environnement**
DE	**LIFE**	**Finanzierungsinstrument für die Umwelt**
RU	**-**	**Финансовый инструмент для окружающей среды**
		программа ЕС по оказанию финансового содействия мероприятиям по охране окружающей среды в странах-членах

350

EN	**LINGUA**	**Action programme to promote foreign language competence in the European Community**
FR	**LINGUA**	**Programme d'action visant à promouvoir la connaissance des langues étrangères dans la Communauté européenne**
DE	**LINGUA**	**Programm zur Förderung der Fremdsprachenkenntnisse in der Europäischen Gemeinschaft**
RU	**ЛИНГВА**	**Программа содействия изучению иностранных языков в Европейском сообществе**

351
EN	LLGDS	landlocked and other geographically disadvantaged States
FR	LLGDS	Etats sans littoral et autres Etats géographiquement désavantagés
DE	LLGDS	Binnenstaaten und andere durch ihre geographische Lage benachteiligte Staaten
RU	-	страны, не имеющие выхода к морю, и другие неблагополучные в географическом отношении страны

352
EN	LSI	large-scale integration
FR	LSI	intégration à grande échelle
DE	LSI	Grossintegration; hohe Integrationsdichte; Grossschaltungsintegrierung
RU	-	широкомасштабная интеграция

353
EN	LUIC	Local Urban Initiative Centres
FR	CIUL	centres d'initiatives urbaines locales
DE	CIUL	Lokale Zentren für städtische Initiativen
RU	-	центры информации о стратегии Сообщества по развитию городов

354
EN	MAGP	multiannual guidance programme
FR	POP	programme d'orientation pluriannuel
DE	MAP	Mehrjähriges Ausrichtungsprogramm
RU	-	многолетняя структурная программа

355
EN	MAST	Marine Science and Technology; Specific Research and Technological Development Programme in the field of Marine Science and Technology
FR	MAST	Programme spécifique de recherche et de développement technologique dans le domaine des sciences et technologies marines
DE	MAST	Spezifisches Programm für Forschung und Entwicklung im Bereich der Meereswissenschaft und -technologie
RU	МАСТ	Наука о море и технология; Специальная научно-техническая программа в области науки о море и морской технологии
		ЕС

356
| EN | MATTHAEUS | Programme of Community Action on the subject of the Vocational Training of Customs Officials |

FR	MATTHAEUS	Programme d'action communautaire en matière de formation professionnelle des fonctionnaires des douanes
DE	MATTHAEUS	Gemeinschaftliches Aktionsprogramm zur beruflichen Aus- und Forbidung der Zollbeamten
RU	-	Программа действий Сообщества по профессиональной подготовке таможенных служащих

357

EN	MCA	monetary compensatory amounts
FR	MCM	montants compensatoires monétaires
DE	WAB	Währungsausgleichsbeträge
RU	-	валютные уравнительные суммы
		доплаты (скидки) к единым гарантированным ценам ЕС на сельскохозяйственные товары, применяемые с целью нейтрализации колебаний курсов валют стран-членов

358

EN	MEDA	Financial cooperation with the Mediterranean third countries
FR	MEDA	Coopération financière de l'UE avec les pays tiers méditerranéens
DE	-	Aktionsprogramm zur finanziellen Zusammenarbeit mit dritten Mittelmeerländer
RU	-	Программа финансового сотрудничества со средиземноморскими странами, не входящими в ЕС *ЕС*

359

EN	MEDIA	Action Programme to Promote the Development of the European Audiovisual Industry
FR	MEDIA	Mesures pour encourager le développement de l'industrie audiovisuelle; Programme d'action pour encourager le développement de l'industrie audiovisuelle européenne
DE	MEDIA	Aktionsprogramm zur Förderung der Entwicklung der europäischen audiovisuellen Industrie
RU	МЕДИА	Программа содействия развитию европейской аудиовизуальной промышленности *ЕС*

360

EN	MEI	main economic indicators
FR	PIE	principaux indicateurs économiques
DE	-	wichtige Wirtschaftsindikatoren
RU	-	основные экономические показатели

361
EN	**MEP**	Member of the European Parliament
FR	-	membre du Parlement européen
DE	-	Mitglied des europäischen Parlament
RU	-	член Европейского Парламента

362
EN	**MERCOSUR**	Southern Cone Common Market
FR	**MERCOSUR**	Marché commun du Sud (Marché commun du Cône sud-americain)
DE	**MERCOSUR**	Südamerikanischer gemeinsame Markt
RU	**МЕРКОСУР**	Южноамериканский общий рынок

363
EN	**MFA**	Multifibre Arrangement; Arrangement regarding International Trade in Textiles
FR	**AMF**	arrangement multifibres; Arrangement concernant le commerce international des textiles
DE	**MFA; WTA**	Allfaservereinbarung; Multifaserabkommen; Welttextilabkommen; Vereinbarung über den internationalen Handel mit textilien
RU	**МТТ**	Соглашение по международной торговле текстилем *(заключено под эгидой ГАТТ)*

364
EN	**MFN**	most favoured nation
FR	**NPF**	nation la plus favorisée
DE	-	Meistbegünstigung
RU	**РНБ**	режим наиболее благоприятствуемой нации; режим наибольшего благоприятствования

365
EN	**MIGA**	Multilateral Investment Guarantee Agency
FR	**AMGI**	Agence multilatérale de garantie des investissements
DE	**MIGA**	Multilaterale Agentur für Investitionsgarantie
RU	**МАИГ**	Международное агентство по инвестиционным гарантиям

366
EN	**MISSOC**	Community Information System on Social Protection
FR	**MISSOC**	Système d'information communautaire sur la protection sociale
DE	**MISSOC**	Informationssystem der Gemeinschaft zum Sozialschutz
RU	-	Информационная система Сообщества по социальной защите

367
EN	**MNE; MNC**	multinational enterprise; multinational corporation
FR	**EMN**	entreprise multinationale

DE	-	multinationales Unternehmen
RU	МНК	многонациональная компания

368
EN	MOU	memorandum of understanding
FR	DCI	déclaration commune d'intention
DE	GA	gemeinsame Absichtserklärung
RU	-	совместная декларация о намерениях

369
EN	MS	Member State
FR	EM	Etat membre
DE	MS	Mitgliedstaat
RU	-	государство-член

370
EN	MSI	medium-Scale integration
FR	MSI	intégration à moyenne échelle
DE	MSI	integrierte Schaltung mittlerer Grösse
RU	-	среднемасштабная интеграция

371
EN	MSP	minimum safeguard price
FR	MSP	prix minimum de sauvegarde
DE	MSP	Mindestschutzpreis
RU	-	минимальная защитная цена

372
EN	MTC; MNC	Mediterranean third countries; Mediterranean non-member countries
FR	PTM	pays tiers méditerranéens
DE	DLM	Drittländer im Mittelmeerraum
RU	-	средиземноморские третьи страны
		страны Средиземноморья, не входящие в ЕС

373
EN	MTN	multilateral trade negotiations
FR	NCM	négociations commerciales multilatérales
DE	MHV	Multilaterale Handelsverhandlungen
RU	МТП	многосторонние торговые переговоры
		(в рамках ГАТТ/ ВТО)

374
EN	NACC	North Atlantic Co-operation Council
FR	COCONA	Conseil de coopération nord-atlantique
DE	NACC; NAKR	Nordatlantischer Kooperationsrat
RU	-	Совет НАТО

375

EN	NACE	General Industrial Classification of Economic Activities within the European Communities
FR	NACE	Nomenclature générale des activités économiques dans les Communautés européennes
DE	NACE	Allgemeine Systematik der Wirtschaftszweige in den Europäischen Gemeinschaften
RU	-	Общая номенклатура видов экономической деятельности в Европейских сообществах

376

EN	NAFO	Northwest Atlantic Fisheries Organization
FR	NAFO; OPANO	Organisation des pêches de l'Atlantique du Nord-Ouest
DE	NAFO	Organisation für die Fischerei im Nordwestatlantik
RU	-	Организация по рыболовству в Северо-западной Атлантике

377

EN	NAFTA	North American Free Trade Agreement
FR	ALENA	Accord de libre-échange nord-américain
DE	NAFTA	Nordamerikanisches Freihandelsabkommen
RU	НАФТА	Соглашение о свободной торговле в Северной Америке

378

EN	NAFTA	North American Free Trade Area
FR	-	zone de libre-échange nord-américaine
DE	NAFTA	Nordamerikanische Freihandelszone
RU	НАФТА	североамериканская зона свободной торговли

379

EN	NATO	North Atlantic Treaty Organization
FR	OTAN	Organisation du traité de l'Atlantique du Nord
DE	NATO	Nordatlantikvertragsorganisation
RU	НАТО	Организация Североатлантического договора; Североатлантический союз

380

EN	NCE	non-compulsory expenditure
FR	DNO	dépenses non obligatoires
DE	NOA	nicht obligatorische Ausgaben
RU	-	необязательные расходы (в бюджете ЕС)

381

EN	NCI	new Community instrument
FR	NIC	nouvel instrument communautaire
DE	NGI	neues Gemeinschaftsinstrument

RU   НИС   новый инструмент Сообщества
                      (по предоставлению займов и кредитов)

382
EN   NCPI   New Commercial Policy Instrument
FR   NIPC   nouvel instrument de politique commerciale
DE   -   neues Instrument für Handelspolitik
RU   -   новый инструмент торговой политики
                      ЕС

383
EN   NEA   Nuclear Energy Agency
FR   AEN   Agence pour l'énergie nucléaire
DE   NEA   Kernenergie-Agentur
RU   АЯЭ   Агентство по ядерной энергии
                      ОЭСР

384
EN   NEAFC   Northeast Atlantic Fisheries Convention
FR   NEAFC   Convention sur les pêcheries de l'Atlantique Nord-Est
DE   NEAFC   Übereinkommen über die Fischerei im Nordostatlantik
RU   НЕАФК   Конвенция по рыболовству в Северо-восточной
                      Атлантике

385
EN   NGDO   non-governmental development organization
FR   ONGD   organisation non gouvernementale de développement
DE   -   Nichtregierungsorganisation für Entwicklung
RU   -   неправительственная организация развития
                      (для содействия развивающимся странам)

386
EN   NGO   non-governmental organization
FR   ONG   organisation non gouvernementale
DE   NRO; NGO   Nichtregierungsorganisation; nichtstaatliche
                      Organisation
RU   НПО   неправительственная организация

387
EN   NI   Non-attached Members
FR   NI   non-inscrits
DE   NI   fraktionslos
RU   -   независимые
                      депутаты Европейского Парламента, не
                      присоединившиеся ни к одной из фракций

388
EN   NIC   newly industrializing countries

FR	**NPI; PNI**	nouveaux pays industrialisés; pays nouvellement industrialisés
DE	**-**	Schwellenländer
RU	**НИС**	новые индустриальные страны

389

EN	**NICE**	Nomenclature of the Industries in the European Communities
FR	**NICE**	Nomenclature des industries établies dans les Communautés européennes
DE	**NICE**	Systematik der Zweige des produzierenden Gewerbes in den Europäischen Gemeinschaften
RU	**-**	Номенклатура отраслей промышленности в Европейских сообществах

390

EN	**NIMEXE**	Nomenclature of Goods for the External Trade Statistics of the Community and Statistics of Trade between Member States
FR	**NIMEXE**	Nomenclature des marchandises pour les statistiques du commerce extérieur de la Communauté et du commerce entre ses Etats membres
DE	**NIMEXE**	Warenverzeichnis für die Statistik des Aussenhandels der Gemeinschaft und des Handels zwischen ihren Mitgliedstaaten
RU	**НИМЭКС**	Номенклатура товаров для внешнеторговой статистики Сообщества и статистики торговли между государствами-членами

391

EN	**NIS**	newly independent States
FR	**NEI**	nouveaux Etats indépendants
DE	**NUS**	neue unabhängige Staaten
RU	**-**	новые независимые государства *бывшие республики СССР*

392

EN	**NIT**	new information technology
FR	**NTI**	nouvelles technologies de l'information
DE	**NIT**	Neue Informationstechnologien
RU	**-**	новая информационная технология

393

EN	**NPCI**	national programme of Community interest
FR	**PNIC**	programme national d'intérêt communautaire
DE	**PNIC**	nationales Programm von gemeinschaftlichem Interesse

RU	-	национальная программа, представляющая интерес для Сообщества в целом

394

EN	NPT	Non-Proliferation Treaty; Treaty on the Non-proliferation of Nuclear Weapons
FR	TNP	Traité de non-prolifération; Traité sur la non-prolifération des armes nucléaires
DE	ASV; NVV	Atomsperrvertrag; Atomwaffensperrvertrag; Vertrag über die Nichtverbreitung von Kernwaffen
RU	-	Договор о нераспространении ядерного оружия

395

EN	NRSE	new and renewable sources of energy
FR	SENR	sources d'énergie nouvelles et renouvelables
DE	NRSE	neue und erneuerbare Energiequellen
RU	-	новые и возобновляемые источники энергии

396

EN	NST	Uniform Nomenclature of Goods for Transport Statistics
FR	NST	Nomenclature uniforme des marchandises pour les statistiques de transport
DE	NST	Einheitliches Güterverzeichnis für die Verkehrsstatistik
RU	-	Унифицированная номенклатура товаров для транспортной статистики

397

EN	NT	national treatment
FR	TN	traitement national
DE	-	nationale Behandlung
RU	HP	национальный режим

398

EN	NTB	non-tariff barriers
FR	-	entraves non tarfaires
DE	-	nichttarifäre Hemmnisse
RU	НТБ	нетарифные барьеры

399

EN	NVA	net value added
FR	VAN	valeur ajoutée nette
DE	-	Nettowertschöpfung
RU	-	чистая добавленная стоимость

400

EN	OAS	Organization of American States
FR	OEA	Organisation des Etats américains

DE	OAS	Organisation Amerikanischer Staaten
RU	ОАГ	Организация американских государств

401

EN	OAU	Organization of African Unity
FR	OUA	Organisation de l'unité africaine
DE	OAU	Organisation der afrikanischen Einigkeit
RU	ОАЕ	Организация африканского единства

402

EN	OCAS	Organization of Central American States
FR	ODECA	Organisation des Etats centraméricains
DE	OCAS	Organisation Zentralamerikanischer Staaten
RU	ОЦАГ	Организация центральноамериканских государств

403

EN	OCT	Overseas Countries and Territories
FR	PTOM	pays et territoires d'outre-mer
DE	ÜLG	überseeische Länder und Gebiete
RU	-	заморские страны и территории

404

EN	OD	French Overseas Departments
FR	DOM	départements d'outre-mer
DE	ÜD	überseeische Departements
RU	-	заморские департаменты Франции

405

EN	ODA	official development assistance
FR	APD	aide publique au développement
DE	ODA	öffentliche Entwicklungshilfe
RU	-	государственная помощь развитию

406

EN	OECD	Organization for Economic Co-operation and Development
FR	OCDE	Organisation de coopération et de développement économiques
DE	OECD	Organisation für wirtschaftliche Zusammenarbeit und Entwicklung
RU	ОЭСР	Организация экономического сотрудничества и развития

407

EN	OHIM	Office for Harmonization in the Internal Market (trade marks)
FR	OHMI	Office de l'harmonisation dans le marché intérieur (marques)

DE	-	**Büro für Harmonisierung auf dem Innenmarkt (Warenzeichen)**
RU	-	**Бюро по гармонизации на внутреннем рынке (товарные знаки)**
		EC

408

EN	OICVP	**Veterinary and Phitosanitary Inspection Office**
FR	OICVP	**Office d'inspection vétérinaire et phytosanitaire**
DE	-	**Verwaltung für die Veterinär- und Phytosanitätskontrolle**
RU	-	**Управление ветеринарного и фитосанитарного контроля**
		EC

409

EN	OJ	**Official Journal (of the European Communities)**
FR	JO	**Journal officiel (des Communautés européennes)**
DE	ABL	**Amtsblatt (der Europäischen Gemeinschaften)**
RU	-	**Официальный вестник (Европейских сообществ)**

410

EN	OMA	**orderly marketing arrangement**
FR	ACO	**arrangement de commercialisation ordonnée**
DE	-	**Abkommen über das Marktordnen**
RU	-	**соглашение об упорядочении рынка**

411

EN	ONP	**Open Network Provision**
FR	ONP	**offre de réseau ouvert de télécommunication**
DE	ONP	**offener Netzzugang**
RU	-	**обеспечение открытого доступа к сетям телекоммуникаций**
		программа ЕС по созданию единого рынка телекоммуникационных услуг

412

EN	OPA	**outward processing arrangements**
FR	RPP	**régime de perfectionnement passif**
DE	PVV	**passiver Veredelungsverkehr**
RU	-	**режим вывоза товара для переработки за границей**
		(с последующим ввозом)

413

EN	OPEC	**Organization of the Petroleum Exporting Countries**
FR	OPEP	**Organisation des pays exportateurs de pétrole**
DE	OPEC	**Organisation der Erdöl exportierenden Länder**
RU	ОПЕК	**Организация стран-экспортеров нефти**

414
EN	**OPT**	**outward processing traffic**
FR	**TPP**	**trafic de perfectionnement passif**
DE	**PVV**	**passiver Veredelungsverkehr**
RU	**-**	вывоз товара для переработки за границей

415
EN	**OSCE**	**Organization for Security and Co-operation in Europe**
FR	**OSCE**	**Organisation pour la sécurité et la coopération en Europe**
DE	**OSZE**	**Organisation für Sicherheit und Zusammenarbeit in Europa**
RU	**ОБСЕ**	**Организация по безопасности и сотрудничеству в Европе**

416
EN	**PACE**	**Community action programme for improving the efficiency of electricity use**
FR	**PACE**	**Programme d'action communautaire visant à améliorer l'efficacité de l'utilisation de l'électricité**
DE	**PACE**	**Aktionsprogramm der Gemeinschaft zur Erhöhung der Effizienz bei der Elektrizitätsverwendung**
RU	**ПЕЙС**	**Программа действий Сообщества по повышению эффективности использования электроэнергии**

417
EN	**PC**	**Programme Committee**
FR	**PC**	**comité du programme**
DE	**PC**	**Planungsausschuss**
RU	**-**	комитет по программе *комитет, занимающийся реализацией программы ЕС*

418
EN	**PCA; APC**	**Partnership and Co-operation Agreement; Agreement on Partnership and Co-operation**
FR	**APC**	**accord de partenariat et de coopération**
DE	**-**	**Abkommen über die Partnerschaft und Zusammenarbeit**
RU	**СПС**	соглашение о партнерстве и сотрудничестве

419
EN	**PCT**	**Patent Co-operation Treaty**
FR	**PCT**	**traité de coopération en matière de brevets**
DE	**PCT**	**Vertrag über die internationale Zusammenarbeit auf dem Gebiet des Patentwesens**
RU	**-**	договор о патентном сотрудничестве

420
EN	**PDB**	preliminary draft budget
FR	**APB**	avant-projet de budget
DE	**VH**	Haushaltsplanvorentwurf; Vorentwurf des Haushaltsplans
RU	-	предварительный проект бюджета *ЕС*

421
EN	**PETRA**	Action Programme for the Vocational Training of Young People and their Preparation for Adult and Working Life
FR	**PETRA**	Programme d'action pour la formation professionnelle des jeunes et la préparation des jeunes à la vie adulte et professionnelle
DE	**PETRA**	Aktionsprogramm für die Berufsausbildung Jugendlicher und zur Vorbereitung der Jugendlichen auf das Erwachsenen- und Erwerbsleben
RU	**ПЕТРА**	Программа действий по профессиональному обучению и подготовке молодежи к взрослой жизни и работе *ЕС*

422
EN	**PFP**	Partnership for Peace
FR	**PFP**	Partenariat pour la paix
DE	-	Partnerschaft für Frieden
RU	-	Партнерство во имя мира *программа НАТО для европейских стран, не участвующих в этой организации*

423
EN	**PHARE**	European Union Programme Providing Grant Finance to Support its Partner Countries in Central Europe to the Stage where They Are Ready to Assume the Obligations of European Union Membership
FR	**PHARE**	Programme de l'Union européenne qui apporte un soutien financier à ses pays partenaires d'Europe centrale afin de les aider à atteindre le niveau de développement des pays de l'Union européenne dans la perspective de leur future adhésion
DE	**PHARE**	Europäische Union Programm, das mit Hilfe von kostenlosen Zuschüssen die Entwicklung seiner Partnerländer in Mitteleuropa unterstützt, bis sie die Anforderungen einer Mitgliedschaft in der Europäischen Union auf sich nehmen können
RU	**ФАРЕ**	Программа Европейского Союза по оказанию финансовой помощи странам-партнерам в Центральной Европе для повышения уровня их развития в перспективе вступления в ЕС

424

EN	PPE	Group of the European People's Party (Christian-Democratic Group)
FR	PPE	groupe du Parti populaire européen (groupe démocrate-chrétien)
DE	PPE	Fraktion der Europäischen Volkspartei (christlich-demokratische Fraktion)
RU	-	группа Европейской народной партии (христианские демократы) *фракция в Европейском Парламенте*

425

EN	PPP	pollutor-pays-principle
FR	PPP	principe du pollueur payeur
DE	-	Verursacherprinzip
RU	-	принцип "виновник загрязнения платит"

426

EN	PPP	purchasing power parity
FR	PPA	parité du pouvoir d'achat
DE	KKP	Kaufkraftparität
RU	-	паритет покупательной силы валют *покупательная способность валюты, определяемая путем сопоставления цен в двух или нескольких странах*

427

EN	PPS	purchasing-power standard
FR	SPA	standard de pouvoir d'achat
DE	KKS	Kaufkraftstandard
RU	-	уровень покупательной способности

428

EN	PRISMA	Community Initiative concerning the Preparation of Businesses for the Single Market
FR	PRISMA	Initiative communautaire concernant la préparation des entreprises dans la perspective du marché unique
DE	PRISMA	Gemeinschaftsinitiative zur Vorbereitung der Unternehmen auf dem Binnenmarkt
RU	-	Инициатива Сообщества по подготовке предприятий к единому рынку *программа ЕС*

429

EN	PSE	Group of the Party of the European Socialists
FR	PSE	groupe du Parti des socialistes européens
DE	PSE	Fraktion der Sozialdemokratischen Partei Europas
RU	-	группа Партии европейских социалистов *фракция в Европейском Парламенте*

430
EN	QR	quantitative restrictions
FR	RQ	restrictions quantitatives
DE	-	mengenmässige Beschränkungen
RU	-	количественные ограничения

431
EN	R	regulation
FR	R	règlement
DE	VO	Verordnung
RU	-	регламент

нормативный акт органов ЕС (Совета, Комиссии), имеющий силу закона и обязательный для всех стран-членов

432
EN	RACE	Research and Development in Advanced Communications Technologies in Europe
FR	RACE	Recherche et développement sur les technologies de pointe dans le domaine des télécommunications en Europe
DE	RACE	Gemeinschaftsprogramm auf dem Gebiet der Telekomunikationstechnologien
RU	РЭЙС	Исследования и разработки в области передовой технологии средств связи в Европе

программа ЕС в области технологии телекоммуникаций

433
EN	R&D	research and technological development
FR	R & D	recherche et développement technologique
DE	F & E	Forchung und technologische Entwicklung
RU	НИОКР	научно-исследовательские и опытно-конструкторские разработки

434
EN	RECHAR	Community Initiative concerning the Economic Conversion of Coal-mining Areas
FR	RECHAR	Initiative communautaire concernant la reconversion économique des bassins charbonniers
DE	RECHAR	Gemeinschaftsinitiative zur wirtschaftlichen Umstrukturierung der Kohlereviere
RU	-	Инициатива Сообщества по экономической конверсии угольных бассейнов

программа ЕС

435

EN	**RECITE**	Regions and Cities for Europe
FR	**RECITE**	Régions et villes d'Europe
DE	**RECITE**	Regionen und Städte Europas
RU	-	Регионы и города Европы

программа сотрудничества между регионами и городами ЕС

436

EN	**REGIS**	Community Initiative concerning the Most Remote Regions
FR	**REGIS**	Initiative communautaire concernant les régions ultrapériphériques
DE	**REGIS**	Gemeinschaftsinitiative zugunsten der Regionen in extremer Randlage
RU	-	Инициатива Сообщества в отношении наиболее удаленных регионов

программа развития заморских территорий и департаментов стран ЕС

437

EN	**REITOX**	European Information Network on Drugs and Drug Addiction
FR	**REITOX**	Réseau européen d'information sur les drogues et les toxicomanies
DE	**REITOX**	Europäisches Informationsnetz für Drogen und Drogensucht
RU	**РЕИТОКС**	Европейская система информации о наркотиках и наркомании

программа ЕС

438

EN	**RETEX**	Community Initiative for Regions Heavily Dependent on the Textiles and Clothing Sector
FR	**RETEX**	Initiative communautaire concernant les régions fortement dépendantes du secteur textile-habillement
DE	**RETEX**	Gemeinschaftsinitiative zugunsten der vom Textil- und Bekleidungssektor stark abhängigen Regionen
RU	-	Инициатива Сообщества для регионов с высокой зависимостью от текстильной и швейной промышленности

программа ЕС

439

EN	**REWARD**	Recycling of Waste R&D
FR	**REWARD**	Recyclage des déchets
DE	**REWARD**	Rückführung von Abfällen

RU - Исследования и разработки по проблемам
рециклирования отходов
программа ЕС

440
EN **RF** Russian Federation
FR - Fédération de Russie
DE - Russische Föderation
RU **РФ** Российская Федерация

441
EN **RGMS** Representatives of the Governments of the Member
States
FR **RGEM** représentants des gouvernements des Etats membres
DE **VRMSt** Vertreter der Regierungen der Mitgliedstaaten
RU - Представители правительств стран-членов

442
EN **SAD** single administrative document
FR **DAU; DU** document administratif unique; document unique
DE - Einheitspapier
RU **ЕАД** единый административный документ
*унифицированная форма таможенной декларации при
импорте в ЕС из третьих стран*

443
EN **SAF** structural-adjustment facility
FR **FAS** facilité d'ajustement structurel
DE **SAF** Strukturanpassungsfazilität
RU - финансовый инструмент структурной перестройки

444
EN **SAVE** Specific Actions for Vigorous Energy Efficiency
FR **SAVE** Actions déterminées en faveur d'une plus grande
efficacité énergétique
DE **SAVE** Entschiedene Aktionen für eine effizientere
Energienutzung
RU **СЭЙВ** Специальная программа действий по повышению
эффективности использования энергии
ЕС

445
EN **SCA** Special Committee on Agriculture
FR **CSA** Comité spécial de l'agriculture
DE **SAL** Sonderausschuss Landwirtschaft
RU - Специальный комитет по сельскому хозяйству
ЕС

446
EN SCIENCE   Programme Plan to Stimulate the International Co-
                    operation and Interchange Needed by European
                    Research Scientists
FR SCIENCE   Plan-programme de stimulation des coopérations
                    internationales et des échanges nécessaires aux
                    chercheurs européens
DE SCIENCE   Plan für die Stimulierung der internationalen
                    Zusammenarbeit und des für die europäischen
                    Forscher notwendigen wissenschaftlichen Austauschs
RU САЙЕНС   План действий по стимулированию
                    международного сотрудничества и обменов,
                    необходимых для европейских исследователей
                    программа ЕС

447
EN SDC; CSD   Sustainable Development Commission; Commission on
                    Sustainable Development
FR CDD   Commission de développement durable
DE SDC   Kommission für umweltverträgliche Entwicklung
RU -   Комиссия по поддержке развития
                    ООН

448
EN SDR   special drawing rights
FR DTS   droits de tirage spéciaux
DE SZR   Sonderziehungsrechte
RU СДР   специальные права заимствования
                    МВФ

449
EN SE   European Company
FR SE; SAE   société européenne; société anonyme européenne
DE SE   Europäische Aktiengesellschaft
RU -   европейская компания
                    форма сотрудничества между предприятиями
                    нескольких стран ЕС

450
EN SEA   Single European Act
FR AUE   Acte unique européen
DE EEA   Einheitliche Europäische Akte
RU EEA   Единый европейский акт

451
EN SGP; GSP   System of Generalized Preferences; Generalized
                    System of Preferences; Generalized Preferences
                    Scheme

FR	SPG	système de préférences généralisées; système généralisé de préférences
DE	APS	allgemeines Präferenzsystem
RU	ОСП	Общая система преференций *ЮНКТАД*

452

EN	SIS	Schengen Information System
FR	SIS	Système d'information Schengen
DE	SIS	Schengener Informationssystem
RU	-	Шенгенская информационная система *(в рамках Шенгенского соглашения ряда стран ЕС о режиме въезда и выезда)*

453

EN	SITC	Standard International Trade Classification
FR	CTCI	Classification type pour le commerce international
DE	SITC	Internationales Warenverzeichnis für den Aussenhandel
RU	СМТК	Стандартная международная торговая классификация

454

EN	SMEs; SMUs; SMBs	small and medium-sized enterprises; small and medium-sized undertakings; small and medium-sized businesses
FR	PME	petites et moyennes entreprises
DE	KMU	kleine und mittlere Unternehmen
RU	МСП	малые и средние предприятия; предприятия малого бизнеса

455

EN	SMI	small and medium-sized industries
FR	PMEI	petites et moyennes entreprises industrielles
DE	-	kleine und mittlere Industriebetriebe
RU	-	малые и средние промышленные предприятия

456

EN	SPES	European Stimulation Plan for Economic Science
FR	SPES	Plan européen de stimulation de la science économique
DE	SPES	europäischer Plan für die Stimulierung der Wirtschaftswissenschaften
RU	СПЕС	Европейский план стимулирования экономической науки *программа ЕС*

457

EN	SPRINT	Strategic Programme for Innovation and Technology Transfer

FR	**SPRINT**	Programme stratégique pour l'innovation et le transfert de technologies
DE	**SPRINT**	Strategisches Programm für Innovation und Technologietransfer
RU	**СПРИНТ**	Стратегическая программа по стимулированию нововведений и передаче технологии
		EC

458

EN	**SSE**	European Statistical System
FR	**SSE**	Système statistique européen
DE	**SSE**	Europäisches Statistisches System
RU	-	Европейская статистическая система
		EC

459

EN	**STABEX**	(System of) Stabilization of Export Earnings
FR	**STABEX**	(système de) stabilisation des recettes d'exportation
DE	**STABEX**	(System der) Stabilisierung der Ausfuhrerlöse
RU	**СТАБЭКС**	система стабилизации доходов от экспорта *(сельскохозяйственных товаров из стран АКТ в ЕС)*

460

EN	**STAR**	Special Telecommunications Action for Regional Development; Community Programme for the Development of Certain Less-favoured Regions of the Community by Improving Access to Advanced Telecommunications Services
FR	**STAR**	Développement de certaines régions défavorisées de la Communauté par un meilleur accès aux services avancés de télécommunications
DE	-	Aktionsprogramm zur Entwicklung einiger ungünstiger Gebiete der Gemeinschaft durch Beitrittserleichterung zum Markt der gegenwärtigen Telekommunikationsdienste
RU	**СТАР**	Программа развития некоторых неблагополучных регионов Сообщества путем облегчения доступа к рынку современных телекоммуникационных услуг

461

EN	**STEP**	Science and Technology for Environmental Protection
FR	**STEP**	Science et technologie pour la protection de l'environnement
DE	**STEP**	Wissenschaft und Technologie für den Umweltschutz
RU	-	Наука и технология для охраны окружающей среды *программа ЕС*

462

EN	**STMS**	short-term monetary support
FR	**SMCT**	soutien monétaire à court terme
DE	**KWB**	kurzfristiger Währungsbeistand
RU	-	краткосрочная валютная поддержка

463

EN	**STRIDE**	Science and Technology for Regional Innovation and Development in Europe
FR	**STRIDE**	Science et technologie pour l'innovation et le développement régionaux en Europe
DE	**STRIDE**	Wissenschaft und Technologie für regionale Innovationen und Entwicklung in Europa
RU	-	Наука и технология для регионального развития и инноваций в Европе
		программа ЕС

464

EN	**SVC**	Standing Veterinary Committee
FR	**CVP**	Comité vétérinaire permanent
DE	**SVA**	Ständiger Veterinärausschuss
RU	-	Постоянный ветеринарный комитет
EC		

465

EN	**SYSMIN**	Scheme for Mineral Products
FR	**SYSMIN**	système "produits miniers"
DE	**SYSMIN**	Regelung für Bergbauerzeugnisse
RU	**СИСМИН**	система для минерального сырья
		поддержание производства и экспорта минерального сырья из стран АКТ в ЕС

466

EN	**TABD**	Transatlantic Business Dialogue
FR	**TABD**	Dialogue économique transatlantique
DE	-	Transatlantischer geschäftlicher Dialog
RU	-	Трансатлантический деловой диалог
		(между ЕС и США)

467

EN	**TAC**	total allowable catch
FR	**TAC**	total admissible des captures; total des captures permises
DE	**TAC**	zulässige Gesamtfangmenge
RU	-	общий допустимый объем вылова рыбы
		(странами-членами в общей рыболовной зоне ЕС)

468

EN	Tacis	European Union Programme Providing Grant Finance for Know-how to Foster the Development of Market Economies and Democratic Societies in the New Independent States and in Mongolia
FR	Tacis	Programme de l'Union européenne ayant pour objectif de financer l'apport de savoir-faire dans le cadre de projets à soutenir le développement d'une économie de marché et de sociétés démocratiques dans les nouveaux Etats indépendants et la Mongolie
DE	Tacis	Europäische Union Programm, das nicht rückzahlbare Zuschüsse für die Vermittlung von Know-how zur Verfügung stellt, um die Entwicklung von Marktwirtschaft und Demokratie in den Neuen Unabhängigen Staaten und der Mongolei zu fördern
RU	Тасис	Программа Европейского Союза в целях содействия развитию рыночной экономики и демократии в странах СНГ и Монголии путем безвозмездного предоставления ноу-хау

469

EN	TARIC	Integrated Tariff of the European Community
FR	TARIC	tarif douanier intégré des Communautés européennes
DE	TARIC	Integrierter Zolltarif der Europäischen Gemeinschaften
RU	ТАРИК	интегрированный тариф Европейских сообществ

470

EN	TBT	technical barriers to trade
FR	ETE	entraves techniques aux échanges
DE	-	technische Schranken im Handel
RU	-	технические барьеры в торговле

471

EN	TCA	Trade and Co-operation Agreement
FR	-	accord commercial et de coopération
DE	-	Handels- und Zusammenarbeitsabkommen
RU	-	соглашение о торговле и сотрудничестве

472

EN	TDB	Trade and Development Board
FR	CCD	Conseil du commerce et du développement
DE	-	Handels- und Entwicklungsrat
RU	-	Совет по торговле и развитию ЮНКТАД

473

EN	TEDIS	Trade Electronic Data Interchange System

FR	TEDIS	Système de transfert électronique de données à usage commercial
DE	TEDIS	elektronischer Datentransfer für kommerzielle Zwecke
RU	-	Система электронного обмена данными о торговле *программа ЕС*

474
EN	TELECOM	EU Telecommunications Council
FR	TELECOM	Conseil télécommunications de l'UE
DE	TELECOM	EU Ministerial Telekommunikationsrat
RU	ТЕЛЕКОМ	Совет ЕС в составе министров телекоммуникаций

475
EN	TELEMAN	Research and Training Programme for the European Atomic Energy Community in the field of Remote Handling in Hazardous or Disordered Nuclear Environments
FR	TELEMAN	Programme de recherche et de formation pour la Communauté européenne de l'énergie atomique dans le domaine de la télémanipulation dans les environnements nucléaires dangereux et perturbés
DE	TELEMAN	Forschungs- und Ausbildungsprogramm für die Europäische Atomgemeinschaft auf dem Gebiet fernbedienter Handhabungssysteme zum Einsatz im Bereich der Kernenergie im Katastrophenschutz und in unbekanntem Umfeld
RU	ТЕЛЕМАН	Программа исследований и обучения для Европейского сообщества по атомной энергии по дистанционному управлению производственными процессами в радиоактивных и других опасных зонах

476
EN	TEMPUS	Trans-European Mobility Programme for University Studies; Trans-European Co-operation Scheme for Higher Education
FR	TEMPUS	Programme de mobilité transeuropéenne pour l'enseignement supérieur; Programme transeuropéen de coopération pour l'enseignement supérieur
DE	TEMPUS	Europaweites Mobilitätsprogramm für den Hochschulbereich; Europaweites Programm zur Zusammenarbeit im Hochschulbereich
RU	ТЕМПУС	Программа трансевропейской мобильности для университетских исследований; Программа трансевропейского сотрудничества в сфере высшего образования *программа ЕС по оказанию содействия странам Центральной и Восточной Европы в развитии высшей школы*

477

EN	**TEN**	**trans-European network**
FR	**RTE**	**réseaux transeuropéens**
DE	**TEN**	**transeuropäisches Netz**
RU	**-**	**трансевропейская сеть**
		(транспорт, телекоммуникации)

478

EN	**TEU**	**Treaty on European Union**
FR	**TUE**	**Traité sur l'Union européenne**
DE	**VEU**	**Vertrag über die Europäische Union**
RU	**-**	**Договор о Европейском Союзе**

479

EN	**THERMIE**	**European Technologies for Energy Management**
FR	**THERMIE**	**Technologies européennes pour la maîtrise de l'énergie**
DE	**THERMIE**	**Europäische Technologien für den Umgang mit der Energie**
RU	**ТЕРМИ**	**Европейские технологии по управлению энергией**
		программа ЕС в целях содействия применению новых "рисковых" технологий в области энергии

480

EN	**TIDE**	**Community Technology Initiative for Disabled and Elderly People**
FR	**TIDE**	**Initiative technologique communautaire en faveur des personnes handicapées et des personnes âgées**
DE	**TIDE**	**Technologieinitiative der Gemeinschaft für Behinderte und ältere Menschen**
RU	**ТАЙД**	**Технологическая инициатива Сообщества для инвалидов и престарелых**
		программа ЕС

481

EN	**TIR**	**international carriage of goods by road**
FR	**TIR**	**transport international de marchandises par route**
DE	**TIR**	**internationaler Strassengüterverkehr**
RU	**ТИР**	**международные автодорожные перевозки грузов**

482

EN	**TLA**	**automatic licensing (arrangements)**
FR	**TLA**	**(régime) toute licence accordée**
DE	**TLA**	**(Verfahren der) automatischen Erteilung von Einfuhrdokumenten**
RU	**-**	**режим автоматического лицензирования**

483

EN	**TNC**	**transnational corporation**
FR	**STN**	**société transnationale**

DE	-	transnationales Unternehmen
RU	ТНК	транснациональная компания (корпорация)

484

EN	TPRM	trade-policy review mechanism
FR	MEPC	mécanisme d'examen des politiques commerciales
DE	TPRM	Mechanismus zur Überprüfung der Handelspolitik
RU	МОТС	механизм обзоров торговой политики
		ВТО

485

EN	TRIMs	trade-related investment measures
FR	TRIM	mesures concernant les investissements et liées au commerce
DE	TRIM; TRIMs	handelsbezogene Investitionsmassnahmen
RU	ТРИМС	инвестиционные меры, относящиеся к торговле
		ВТО

486

EN	TRIPs	trade-related aspects of intellectual property rights
FR	ADPIC; TRIPs	aspects des droits de propriété intellectuelle qui touchent au commerce
DE	TRIP; TRIPs	handelsbezogene Aspekte der Rechte des geistigen Eigentums
RU	ТРИПС	торговые аспекты прав на интеллектуальную собственность
		ВТО

487

EN	UA	unit of account
FR	UC	unité de compte
DE	RE	Rechnungseinheit
RU	-	расчетная единица

488

EN	UCLAF	Unit on Co-ordination of Fraud Prevention
FR	UCLAF	unité de coordination de la lutte antifraudes
DE	UCLAF	Dienststelle für die Koordinierung der Massnahmen zur Bekämpfung von Betrügereien
RU	-	Подразделение по борьбе с мошенничеством *(при Европейской Комиссии)*

489

EN	UN; UNO	United Nations; United Nations Organization
FR	ONU	Organisation des Nations unies
DE	VN	Vereinte Nationen
RU	ООН	Объединенные Нации; Организация Объединенных Наций

490

EN	**UNCED**	United Nations Conference on Environment and Development
FR	**CNUED**	Conférence des Nations unies sur l'environnement et le développement
DE	**UNCED**	Konferenz der Vereinten Nationen über Umwelt und Entwicklung
RU	**ЮНСЕД**	Конференция ООН по окружающей среде и развитию

491

EN	**UNCITRAL**	United Nations Commission on International Trade Law
FR	**CNUDCI**	Commission des Nations unies pour le droit commercial international
DE	**UNCITRAL**	Kommission der Vereinten Nationen für internationales Handelsrecht
RU	**ЮНСИТРАЛ**	Комиссия ООН по международному торговому праву

492

EN	**UNCTAD**	United Nations Conference on Trade and Development
FR	**CNUCED**	Conférence des Nations unies pour le commerce et le développement
DE	**UNCTAD; WHK**	Handels- und Entwicklungskonferenz der Vereinten Nationen
RU	**ЮНКТАД**	Конференция ООН по торговле и развитию

493

EN	**UNDP**	United Nations Development Programme
FR	**PNUD**	Programme des Nations unies pour le développement
DE	**UNDP**	Entwicklungsprogramm der Vereinten Nationen
RU	**ПРООН**	Программа развития ООН

494

EN	**UNEP**	United Nations Environmental Programme
FR	**PNUE**	Programme des Nations unies pour l'environnement
DE	**UNEP**	Umweltprogramm der Vereinten Nationen
RU	**ЮНЕП**	Программа ООН по охране окружающей среды

495

EN	**UNESCO**	United Nations Educational, Scientific and Cultural Organization
FR	**UNESCO**	Organisation des Nations unies pour l'éducation, la science et la culture
DE	**UNESCO**	Organisation der Vereinten Nationen für Erziehung, Wissenschaft und Kultur
RU	**ЮНЕСКО**	Организация Объединенных Наций по вопросам образования, науки и культуры

496

EN	**UNGA**	**United Nations General Assembly**
FR	**AGNU**	**Assemblée générale des Nations unies**
DE	**-**	**Generalversammlung der Vereinten Nationen**
RU	**ГА ООН**	**Генеральная Ассамблея Организации Объединенных Наций**

497

EN	**UNICE**	**Union of Industrial and Employers' Confederations of Europe**
FR	**UNICE**	**Union des confédérations de l'industrie et des employeurs d'Europe**
DE	**-**	**Europäische Konfederationsunion der Industriellen und Unternehmer**
RU	**ЮНИСЕ**	**Европейский союз конфедераций промышленников и предпринимателей**
		объединение национальных конфедераций стран ЕС

498

EN	**UNIDO**	**United Nations Industrial Development Organization**
FR	**ONUDI**	**Organisation des Nations unies pour le développement industriel**
DE	**UNIDO**	**Organisation der Vereinten Nationen für industrielle Entwicklung**
RU	**ЮНИДО**	**Организация Объединенных Наций по промышленному развитию**

499

EN	**UPE**	**European Political Union**
FR	**UPE**	**Union politique européene**
DE	**UPE**	**Fraktion Union für Europa**
RU	**-**	**группа "Союз за Европу"**
		фракция в Европейском Парламенте

500

EN	**UR**	**Uruguay Round**
FR	**UR**	**Uruguay-ronde**
DE	**UR**	**Uruguay Runde**
RU	**УР**	**Уругвайский раунд**
		многосторонние торговые переговоры в рамках ГАТТ

501

EN	**USSR**	**Union of Soviet Socialist Republics**
FR	**URSS**	**Union des républiques socialistes soviétiques**
DE	**UdSSR**	**Union der Sozialistischen Sowjet-Republiken**
RU	**СССР**	**Союз Советских Социалистических Республик**

502

EN	V	The Green Group in the European Parliament
FR	V	Groupe des Verts au Parlement européen
DE	V	Fraktion Die Grünen im Europäischen Parlament
RU	-	группа ”Зеленых” в Европейском Парламенте
		фракция в Европейском Парламенте

503

EN	VALUE	Specific Programme for the Dissemination and Utilization of Scientific and Technological Research Results
FR	VALUE	Programme spécifique de diffusion et d'utilisation des résultats de la recherche scientifique et technologique
DE	VALUE	Spezifisches Programm zur Verbreitung und Nutzung der Ergebnisse der wissenschaftlichen und technischen Forschung
RU	ВЭЛЬЮ	Специальная программа по распространению и использованию результатов научно-технических исследований *ЕС*

504

EN	VAT	value-added tax
FR	TVA	taxe sur la valeur ajoutée
DE	MWSt	Mehrwertsteuer
RU	НДС	налог на добавленную стоимость

505

EN	VER	voluntary export restraint
FR	LVE	limitation volontaire des exportations
DE	VER	freiwillige Ausfuhrbeschränkungen
RU	-	добровольное ограничение экспорта

506

EN	VHSI	very-high-speed integration
FR	VHSI	intégration à très grande vitesse
DE	-	Hochschnellintegration
RU	-	высокоскоростная интеграция

507

EN	VRA	voluntary restraint agreement
FR	-	accord d'autolimitation
DE	VRA	Selbstbeschränkungsabkommen
RU	-	соглашение о добровольном ограничении *(производства/экспорта)*

508

EN	WEU	Western European Union
FR	UEO	Union de l'Europe occidentale

DE	WEU	Westeuropäische Union
RU	ЗЕС	Западноевропейский союз

509

EN	WFP	World Food Programme
FR	PAM	Programme alimentaire mondial
DE	WEP	Welternährungsprogramm
RU	МПП	Мировая продовольственная программа

510

EN	WIPO	World Intellectual Property Organization
FR	OMPI	Organisation mondiale de la propriété intellectuelle
DE	WIPO	Weltorganisation für geistiges Eigentum
RU	ВОИС	Всемирная организация по интеллектуальной собственности
		ООН

511

EN	WTO	World Trade Organization
FR	OMC	Organisation mondiale du commerce
DE	WTO	Welthandelsorganisation
RU	ВТО	Всемирная торговая организация

512

EN	WCO	World Custom Organization
FR	OMD	Organisation mondiale douanière
DE	WZO	Weltzollorganisation
RU	ВТО	Всемирная таможенная организация
		(бывш. Совет таможенного сотрудничества)

513

EN	XRs	export restraints
FR	-	restrictions à l'exportation
DE	-	Exporteinschränkungen
RU	-	экспортные ограничения

514

EN	YES	Youth Exchange Scheme
FR	YES	Echanges de jeunes
DE	-	Aktionsprogramm des Jugendaustausches
RU	-	Программа молодежного обмена
		ЕС

515

EN	YFEC	Youth Forum of the European Communities
FR	FJCE	Forum Jeunesse des Communautés européennes
DE	-	Jugendforum der Europäischen Gemeinschaften
RU	-	Молодежный форум Европейских сообществ

516
EN	**YIO**	**Yearbook of International Organizations**
FR	**AOI**	**Annuaire des organisations internationales**
DE	-	**Jahrbuch der internationalen Organisationen**
RU	-	**Ежегодник международных организаций**

517
EN	**ZSP**	**zone of special protection**
FR	**ZPS**	**zone de protection spéciale**
DE	-	**besonders schutzbedürftiges Gebiet**
RU	-	**зона особой защиты**

INDICES

INDICES

INDIZES

УКАЗАТЕЛИ

General Latin-alphabet Index of Abbreviations
Index général des sigles en alphabet latin
Index der Abkürzungen (in lateinischen Buchstaben)
Сводный указатель английских, французских и немецких сокращений
в порядке латинского алфавита

AA	216		AME	187
AAMS	1		AMF	363
AASM	1		AMGI	365
ABL	409		AMS	17
ACA	2		ANASE	20
ACE	3		AO EPÜ	325
ACE	4		AOI	516
ACE	5		APB	420
ACEA	135		APC	418
ACI	296		APD	405
ACM	6		APEC	18
ACNAT	7		API-PME	16
ACO	410		APS	451
ACP	8		ARA	15
ACP	9		ARE	19
ADN	10		ASE	215
ADPIC	486		ASEAN	20
AdR	103		ASEM	21
ADR	11		ASEUR	22
AE	12		ASSUC	23
AE	130		AStV	105
AEC	131		ASV	394
AEE	168		ATE	225
AEEN	195		AUA	24
AELE	176		AUE	450
AEN	383		AVV	321
AETR	13		AVV	323
AGNU	496		AWTF	115
AGR	14			
AIA	15		BCC	25
AIAI	311		BCE	143
AID	304		BC-NET	26
AIE	306		BCR	43
AIEA	293		BEE	169
AIP	295		BEI	177
AIP-SME	16		BENELUX	27
AIZ	81		BERD	139
AKP	8		BEUC	28
ALA	342		BIC	29
ALADI	345		BIOMED	30
ALALC	344		BIOTECH	31
ALENA	377		BIP	275

ERC	210	Europol	249
ERC	211	EUROS	250
ERDF	212	EUROSTAT	251
ERE	232	EUROTECNET	252
ERGO	213	EUROTRA	253
ERM	214	EURYDICE	254
ERZ	211	EUTELSAT	255
E/S	319	EUVP	256
ESA	215	EVCA	257
ESA	216	EVG	162
ESA	217	EVS	149
ESB	37	EWA	187
ESC	218	EWG	170
ESC	157	EWI	190
ESCB	219	EWIV	172
ESF	220	EWO	215
ESF	221	EWR	167
ESPRI	222	EWRE	193
ESPRIT	223	EWS	220
ESRIN	224	EWS	191
ESVG	217	EYC	258
ETA	225	EYF	259
ETC	226	EZB	143
ETE	470	EZBS	219
ETS	227		
ETSC	228	FADN	260
ETSI	229	FAO	261
ETUC	230	FAS	443
EU	231	FAST	262
EUA	232	FDI	263
EuGH	87	FEACVT	175
EUI	233	FEC	147
EURAM	234	FECOM	189
EURATOM	133	FED	164
EUREKA	235	FEDER	212
EURES	236	FEI	179
EURESCOM	237	FEJ	259
EURET	238	FEOGA	134
EURISTOTE	239	FES	220
EUROCHAMBRES	240	FFC	77
EUROCONTROL	241	FFCFI	51
EURO COOP	242	FHZ	269
EUROCOPI	243	FIAF	264
EUROCOTON	244	FIFG	264
EUROFER	245	FJCE	515
EUROFORM	246	FLAIR	265
EuronAid	247	FMI	313
EUROPECHE	248	FOD	266

Index of Russian Abbreviations
Index des sigles russes
Index der Russischen Abkürzungen
Указатель русских сокращений

ANNEXES

ANNEXES

ANLAGEN

ПРИЛОЖЕНИЯ

I. Member States of the European Union
I. Etats membres de l'Union Européenne
I. Mitgliedstaaten der Europäischen Union
I. Государства-члены Европейского Союза

EN	A	Austria	EN	I	Italy
FR	A	Autriche	FR	I	Italie
DE	A	Österreich	DE	I	Italien
RU	-	Австрия	RU	-	Италия

EN	B	Belgium	EN	L	Luxembourg
FR	B	Belgique	FR	L	Luxembourg
DE	B	Belgien	DE	L	Luxemburg
RU	-	Бельгия	RU	-	Люксембург

EN	DK	Denmark	EN	NL	Netherlands
FR	DK	Danemark	FR	NL	Pays-Bas
DE	DK	Dänemark	DE	NL	Niederlande
RU	-	Дания	RU	-	Нидерланды

EN	FIN	Finland	EN	P	Portugal
FR	FIN	Finlande	FR	P	Portugal
DE	FIN	Finnland	DE	P	Portugal
RU	-	Финляндия	RU	-	Португалия

EN	F	France	EN	E	Spain
FR	F	France	FR	E	Espagne
DE	F	Frankreich	DE	E	Spanien
RU	-	Франция	RU	-	Испания

EN	D	Germany	EN	S	Sweden
FR	D	Allemagne	FR	S	Suède
DE	D	Deutschland	DE	S	Schweden
RU	-	Германия	RU	-	Швеция

EN	GR	Greece	EN	UK	United Kingdom
FR	GR	Grèce	FR	UK	Royaume-Uni
DE	GR	Griechenland	DE	UK	Grossbritannien
RU	-	Греция	RU	-	Великобритания

EN	IRL	Ireland
FR	IRL	Irlande
DE	IRL	Irland
RU	-	Ирландия

*   *   *

EN	EUR 6	Belgium, Federal Republic of Germany, France, Italy, Luxembourg, Netherlands
FR	EUR 6	Belgique, République Fédérale d'Allemagne, France, Italie, Luxembourg, Pays-Bas
DE	EUR 6	Belgien, Die Bundesrepublik Deutschland, Frankreich, Italien, Luxemburg, Niederlande
RU	Европа-6	Бельгия, Федеративная Республика Германии, Франция, Италия, Люксембург, Нидерланды

EN	EUR 9	EUR 6 plus Denmark, Ireland and United Kingdom
FR	EUR 9	EUR 6 plus Danemark, Irlande et Royaume-Uni
DE	EUR 9	EUR 6 plus Dänemark, Irland und Grossbritanien
RU	Европа-9	Европа-6 плюс Дания, Ирландия и Великобритания

EN	EUR 10	EUR 9 plus Greece
FR	EUR 10	EUR 9 plus Grèce
DE	EUR 10	EUR 9 plus Griechenland
RU	Европа-10	Европа-9 плюс Греция

EN	EUR 12	EUR 10 plus Spain and Portugal
FR	EUR 12	EUR 10 plus Espagne et Portugal
DE	EUR 12	EUR 10 plus Spanien und Portugal
RU	Европа-12	Европа-10 плюс Испания и Португалия

EN	EUR 15	EUR 12 plus Austria, Finland and Sweden
FR	EUR 15	EUR 12 plus Autriche, Finlande et Suède
DE	EUR 15	EUR 12 plus Österreich, Finnland und Schweden
RU	Европа-15	Европа-12 плюс Австрия, Финляндия и Швеция

II. National Currencies of the EU Member States, USA and Japan
II. Devises nationales des Etats membres de l'UE, des Etats-Unis et du Japon
II. Nationale Währungen der Mitgliedstaaten der EU, der Vereinigte Staaten von Amerika und Japan
II. Национальные валюты государств-членов ЕС, США и Японии

EN	ÖS	Austrian schilling	EN	DM	German mark
FR	ÖS	schilling autrichien	FR	DM	mark allemand
DE	ÖS	Österreichischer Schilling	DE	DM	Deutsche Mark
RU	шилл.	австрийский шиллинг	RU	нем.м.	немецкая марка

EN	BLF	Belgian franc	EN	DRA	Greek drachma
FR	BLF	franc belge	FR	DRA	drachme grecque
DE	BLF	Belgischer Franken	DE	DRA	Griechische Drachme
RU	б.фр.	бельгийский франк	RU	драхм	греческая драхма

EN	DKR	Danish krone	EN	IRL	Irish pound
FR	DKR	couronne danoise	FR	IRL	livre irlandaise
DE	DKR	Dänische Krone	DE	IRL	Irisches Pfund
RU	д.кр.	датская крона	RU	ирл.ф.	ирландский фунт

EN	HFL	Dutch guilder	EN	LIT	Italian lira
FR	HFL	florin hollandais	FR	LIT	lire italienne
DE	HFL	Niederländischer Gulden	DE	LIT	Italienische Lira
RU	гул.	голландский гульден	RU	ит.л.	итальянская лира

EN	FMK	Finnish mark	EN	LFR	Luxembourg franc
FR	FMK	mark finlandais	FR	LFR	franc luxembourgeois
DE	FMK	Finnische Mark	DE	LFR	Luxemburger Franken
RU	ф.м.	финская марка	RU	л.фр.	люксембургский франк

EN	FF	French franc	EN	ESC	Portuguese escudo
FR	FF	franc français	FR	ESC	escudo portugais
DE	FF	Französischer Franken	DE	ESC	Portugiesischer Eskudo
RU	ф.фр.	французский франк	RU	порт. эск.	португальский эскудо

EN	UKL	Pound sterling	EN	USD	US dollar
FR	UKL	livre sterling	FR	USD	dollar des Etats-Unis
DE	UKL	Pfund Sterling	DE	USD	US Dollar
RU	ф.ст.	английский фунт стерлингов	RU	ам. долл.	доллар США

EN	PTA	Spanish peseta	EN	YEN	Japanese yen
FR	PTA	peseta espagnole	FR	YEN	yen japonais
DE	PTA	Spanische Pesete	DE	YEN	Japanischer Yen
RU	песет	испанская песета	RU	иен	японская иена

EN	SKR	Swedish krona
FR	SKR	couronne suèdoise
DE	SKR	Schwedische Krone
RU	ш.кр.	шведская крона